TEACHING LITERATURE TO ADOLESCENTS: POETRY

STEPHEN DUNNING
University of Michigan

TEACHING
LITERATURE
TO
ADOLESCENTS

SCOTT, FORESMAN AND COMPANY

The author wishes to thank those who have given permission to reprint the following poems: "Absolutes" by Gustave Keyser, from the New Mexico Quarterly, Autumn 1963, XXXIII, No. 3, p. 292. "Apple Peeler," Copyright © 1953 by Robert Francis. Reprinted from The Orb Weaver, by Robert Francis, by permission of Wesleyan University Press. "August from My Desk" by Roland Flint. Copyright © 1965 by The Atlantic Monthly Company, Boston, Mass. Reprinted by permission of the author. "Common Sense of the Crows" by Judson Jerome, from the New Mexico Quarterly, Spring 1958, XXVIII, No. 1, p. 45. An excerpt from "The Cow" from From Time to Time by John Ciardi (New York: Twayne Publishers, Inc., 1951). "Crossing" from Letter from a Distant Land by Philip Booth. Copyright 1953 by Philip Booth. Reprinted by permission of The Viking Press, Inc. "The Crows" by Leah Bodine Drake, from Hawk and Whippoorwill, Autumn 1963. "Dreams," Copyright, 1932, by Alfred A. Knopf, Inc. Renewed, 1950, by Langston Hughes. Reprinted by permission of the publisher from The Dreamkeeper by Langston Hughes. "Farm Boy After Summer," Copyright © 1959 by Robert Francis. Reprinted from The Orb Weaver, by Robert Francis, by permission of Wesleyan University Press. "First Love" by Edith May Alcock, from New Campus Writing II, edited by Nolan Miller. © Copyright 1957 by Bantam Books, Inc., and reprinted by permission of the publisher. All Rights Reserved. "Fisherman" from Letter from a Distant Land by Philip Booth. Copyright 1953 by Philip Booth. Reprinted by permission of The Viking Press, Inc. "The Flat" by Laurence Lieberman, from Harper's Magazine, October 1963, p. 93. "Fueled" from Serve Me a Slice of Moon, © 1965, by Marcie Hans. Reprinted by permission of Harcourt, Brace & World, Inc. An excerpt from "Haying," reprinted from Prairie Schooner by Ethel Romig Fuller by permission of University of Nebraska Press. Copyright 1952 by the University of Nebraska Press. All Rights Reserved. "The Heroes" (Copyright 1950 Garrett Publications) is reprinted with the permission of Charles Scribner's Sons from Good News of Death and Other Poems by Louis Simpson, Poets of Today, II. "High Diver," Copyright © 1953 by Robert Francis. Reprinted from The Orb Weaver, by Robert Francis, by permission of Wesleyan University Press. "Kansas Boy" by Ruth Lechlitner, from Poetry, November 1931, p. 84. "The Loser" by Charles Bukowski, from Sparrow, November 1960, No. 14. An excerpt from "The Love Song of J. Alfred Prufrock" from Collected Poems 1909–1962 by T. S. Eliot, copyright, 1936, by Harcourt, Brace & World, Inc., copyright © 1963 by T. S. Eliot. Reprinted by permission of Harcourt, Brace & World, Inc., and Faber and Faber Limited. "Maine" from The Islanders by Philip Booth. Copyright © 1960 by Philip Booth. Reprinted by permission of The Viking Press, Inc. "Mirror" from The Carpentered Hen and Other Tame Creatures by John Updike. Copyright © 1957 by John Updike. Originally appeared in The New Yorker under the title "Reflection," and reprinted by permission of Harper & Row, Publishers. An excerpt from "The Naming of Parts," A Map of Verona and Other Poems, copyright, 1947, by Henry Reed. Reprinted by permission of Harcourt, Brace & World, Inc., and Jonathan Cape Limited. "Pitcher," Copyright © 1953 by Robert Francis. Reprinted from The Orb Weaver, by Robert Francis, by permission of Wesleyan University Press. "Propeller" from The Islanders by Philip Booth. Copyright © 1959 by Philip Booth. Reprinted by permission of The Viking Press, Inc. "Reflections on a Gift of Watermelon Pickle Received from a Friend called Felicity" by John Tobias, from New Mexico Quarterly, Spring 1961, XXX, No. 1, p. 45. "Sing a Song of Juniper" from The Sound I Listened For by Robert Francis (New York: The Macmillan Company, 1944). Reprinted by permission of the author. "Southbound on the Freeway" (which first appeared in The New Yorker, copyright © 1963 May Swenson) is reprinted with the permission of the author and Charles Scribner's Sons from To Mix With Time by May Swenson. "Summons" from The Sound I Listened For by Robert Francis (New York: The Macmillan Company, 1944). Reprinted by permission of the author. "Sunday Climb" from Letter from a Distant Land by Philip Booth. All Rights Reserved. Reprinted by permission of The Viking Press, Inc. "Swift Things Are Beautiful," reprinted with permission of The Macmillan Company from Away Goes Sally by Elizabeth Coatsworth. Copyright 1934 by The Macmillan Company. Copyright renewed 1962 by Elizabeth Coatsworth Beston. "These Have I Loved" by Barbara Fainstein, from The Horn Book, August 1962, p. 406. An excerpt from "Watching Gymnasts," first published in Syracuse 10. Reprinted by permission of Robert Francis. "Winter Dawn" by R. P. Lister. From The New Yorker, January 30, 1960. © 1960 by New Yorker Magazine, Inc. Reprinted by permission of Ashley Famous Agency, Inc. "Poetry as (Disciplined) Play" by Stephen Dunning, from The English Journal, November 1963, LII, pp. 601–602, 607–609.

Thanks also go to the publishers of the following reference works for permission to reproduce their pages: "Edgar Allan Poe" reprinted from the Encyclopedia Americana by permission of the publishers, Grolier Incorporated, New York, 1962, XXII, pp. 273, 274. From Granger's Index to Poetry, 5th edition, William F. Bernhardt, editor (New York: Columbia University Press, 1962), pp. 308, 1738, 2016. From The Home Book of Quotations, 9th edition, Burton Stevenson, editor (New York: Dodd, Mead & Company, 1958), pp. 238, 2444. From Index to Children's Poetry, Second Supplement, John E. and Sara W. Brewton, editors (Bronx: H. W. Wilson Company, 1965), pp. xvii, 209. "Poetry" and "Edwin Arlington Robinson" reprinted with permission of The Macmillan Company from Literary History of the United States by Robert E. Spiller, editor. Copyright © 1946, 1947, 1948, 1953, 1963 by The Macmillan Company. From The Reader's Encyclopedia, edited by William Rose Benét. Copyright © 1965, 1955, 1948 by Thomas Y. Crowell Company, New York, publishers, p. 1006. From Readers' Guide to Periodical Literature, volume XXII (Bronx: H. W. Wilson Company, March 1961–February 1963), pp. 1468, 1469. From Twentieth Century Authors, First Supplement, Stanley J. Kunitz, editor (Bronx: H. W. Wilson Company, 1955), pp. 612, 613.

Preface

This book is addressed to three fictional people. Two of them are young and will soon graduate from college and soon thereafter begin teaching English. The first, a young lady active in undergraduate politics at Somewhere University, is an English major in the School of Education, carries a "light B average," and finds time for both a substantial social life and the requirements of a work scholarship.

The second, a young man of somewhat serious mien, will graduate from Ivyleague College with some academic honors and the intention to do something important about the teaching of English. He's not so serious as I've made him out to be. He plays good bridge, average poker, and an E-flat alto saxophone. But he is more reserved than many young men. Perhaps the fact that he's in love and wants to get married contributes to his uneasiness about the economics facing him as a teacher of English.

Sometimes, squeezing my eyes shut, I see these two young people as, carefully combed, they sit for their yearbook portraits. Somewhere behind them, in less sharp focus, stands the third person I am addressing—an English teacher of ten years' experience. She's had many successes in teaching, some notable failures. She is vaguely dissatisfied with what has happened the past several years when she's taught poetry to three classes of ninth-grade "regulars" and her honors section of advanced-placement seniors.

This book is for such people as these three.

Three observations about this book may help my audience read it and use it. First, I'm consciously guilty of overstatement. When I argue that America has not treated the poet very well, I sometimes select extreme instances to further my case. I do so because the teaching of poetry has been generally ineffective and because I honestly believe that we can do better as teachers than we do.

The second is that the book is quite free of well-known, long-honored poems; most examples and illustrations are from poems written in the past decade. This emphasis on current poetry is in keeping with my belief that too little of it is taught in junior and senior high schools. Moreover, teachers are usually readier for the teaching of the Shakespearean sonnet or one of Wordsworth's "Lucy" poems than they are for recent poems. If the ideas and principles here are as sound as I believe them to be, they should help the teacher-to-be teach fine old poems as well as new poems.

Third, if the principles of Part One seem stodgy or abstract, look into Parts Four, Two, and Three — in that order. Part Four deals specifically with approaches to poems; it may be a better place to begin, for some readers, than is the consideration of the principles underlying those approaches.

The distinguished contributions to this book are those sections (Parts Two and Three) prepared by two successful poets. I imposed on Robert Francis and Philip Booth this kind of structure: "First say something you believe to be true and important about poetry. Then take some of your poems and talk about them as though you were teaching them in different classrooms." I admit to having selected the poems that Robert Francis and Philip Booth discuss; but what they say about their own poems is almost exactly what they say they *would* say. It has been rewarding, during the years this book has been under way, to get to know these two men, whether personally or by correspondence.

The conventional appreciations to wife, children, publisher, and professional friends obtain here. These appreciations are genuine even though not expressed explicitly. Five friends must be named, however. William Combs read much of the manuscript and contributed trenchant questions and suggestions. Edward Lueders and Hugh L. Smith gave me the needed kick when, four long years ago, this book was only a tentative idea. Mrs. Lee Bernd has worked with the idea of this book in general and with the library materials in particular for many months. Whatever is useful in Part Five must be credited to Mrs. Bernd; what is not useful or accurate must be my own responsibility. Generously and genially, my colleague Alan Howes has read proof, improved sentences, and cheered me when despair threatened.

Stephen Dunning
Ann Arbor
March 31, 1966

Contents

PART ONE

The Teaching of Poetry

"Most Americans do not like poetry," writes Gilbert Highet in *The Powers of Poetry*.[1] "We may respect it, but we do not enjoy it." Highet goes on to say that half a century ago audiences attended performances of symphony music chiefly because they were social events. "Now," Highet says, "we are a nation of music-lovers, collect records of fine music, and have high standards of composition and performance." He concludes that "perhaps fifty or sixty years in the future we shall appreciate poetry in the same way; but now we do not."

Highet is right that most Americans do not enjoy poetry. Not many Americans even read it; and enjoyment is not an inevitable consequence of reading poetry. Enjoyment requires skill in approaching poetry, a sense of what the poet is doing with language, an awareness of how form, image, and sound combine to make meaning. It is here that teachers fail; they teach poetry badly or indifferently or not at all. If they were successful in teaching poetry, the result would be enjoyment. TV would be featuring poetry, students would be buying it, booksellers would be selling it, libraries would be shelving it, and parents would be subscribing to the little magazines. American society, in short, would be demonstrating its appreciation for poetry in the characteristic American way: by paying for it.

The way teachers can improve the reputation of poetry is to improve their teaching of poetry. This book is largely concerned

1. New York: Oxford University Press, 1960.

with principles for teaching poetry, principles that might, taken all together, nudge tomorrow's citizenry from an aversion to poetry to a delight with poetry. Since I hope for a sympathetic reading of the principles, I hazard here a premature digression. I want to indicate poetry's infirm condition and to specify several symptoms of its disrepair. If I can persuade you that poetry presents a special case in the literature program, you might then be persuaded that some rather unorthodox principles should influence how it is taught.

Poetry: a special case

ITEM. From *The New York Times Magazine*, May 2, 1965. Having taken care of high-school teachers ["The teaching of poetry in high schools is bad. Many people who teach in high school have no love for it, and no understanding of poetry—it's just their job"], Louis Simpson accommodates the common citizen:

> . . . Few people think of buying a book of poems, though they may come to poetry-readings. In Denmark a poet can sell thousands of copies.
>
> I suppose they come to poetry-readings to look at the wild animals.
>
> What they really want is romantic behavior. The public that does not read poetry will consume books and news items about poets. I once talked to a woman who was excited by Brinnin's book about Dylan Thomas.
>
> "What a wonderful person!" she said. "I'd like to read everything he's written."
>
> I said, "Well, there are the 'Collected Poems.' Of course, Thomas isn't easy going."
>
> "I don't mean Thomas. I mean John Malcolm Brinnin."

ITEM. From *Newsweek*, November 5, 1962.

> "When you are sitting next to someone at a bar, or on a train, and he asks you 'What's your line?' and you tell him you're a poet, you do so with a certain embarrassment." In these words, Babette Deutsch, poet and translator, defined the poet's place in society. "Worse than that," she added, "he hears you with a certain embarrassment."

Miss Deutsch's personal embarrassment, reported by *Newsweek* from the federally sponsored National Poetry Festival of 1962, was made general by the situation of *Poetry* magazine, honored at the Festival for its fifty years of publication. "Small of circulation (6500—its all-time high) and financially disastrous (annual deficit: $30,000), it is kept alive by sheer will and a sense of obligation to the nation's most ignored art." This is the situation of the magazine that poet Paul Engle called "a professional journal for poets. Publication in *Poetry* for a young man means that he *is* a poet and that it's all right to go on writing poetry."[2]

But, according to *Newsweek*, it was the late Randall Jarrell "who most accurately gauged the situation of the poet."

> His wife's dressmaker in Greensboro, N.C., had told Mrs. Jarrell how wonderful she thought it would be to go to Washington where her husband would "be reading with Jack Frost and all those famous poets."

"Poetry doesn't sell," Jarrell himself lamented. "The trouble is that 90 per cent of the intelligentsia don't bother to read poetry. People have trouble with it because they don't practice reading it enough." (When given his check as National Book poetry winner, *Saturday Review* reports, "Jarrell accepted his check on the platform and promptly put it in his wallet with the comment: 'If I wrote fiction, I wouldn't need to be so careful about this.'")

ITEM. Perhaps the profusion of "little magazines" contradicts the claim that poetry is "the nation's most ignored art." I don't think so. If relevant evidence is available, I haven't found it, but I would *guess* that for every dozen magazines that publish Issue 1 of Volume I, no more than two or three persist into Volume II. Few endure more than several years. In autumn of 1963, after four years' effort, August Derleth had to cease publication of *Hawk & Whippoorwill*. In the final issue of that fine little magazine, Derleth wrote:

> I undertook the publication of *Hawk & Whippoorwill*, determined to bring out at least ten issues, primarily to inquire into the potential public for a magazine which . . . was inclined toward traditional forms. . . .

> Subscribers to the first year of *Hawk & Whippoorwill* numbered approximately two hundred; subscribers to [the fourth year]

2. In June 1965, *Poetry* editor Henry Rago reported an increase to 7450 subscribers; at this rate of growth it will be 1990 before *Poetry* reaches the present paid circulation of the *National Bowlers Journal and Billiard Revue* and sometime in the twenty-first century before it equals the present circulation of the *Canada Poultryman*. (See the *Standard Periodical Directory*, 1964–1965.)

numbered less than half that number, which, I conclude—perhaps erroneously—is not so much criticism of the contents of the magazine as proof of a sad indifference to it. . . .

. . . Basically, there is—as everyone knows—no very great public for poetry in America, in part certainly because so much of the teaching of English in the nation is so uninspired and inept.

"Uninspired" and "inept" are strong enough words. I think they are used precisely here.

ITEM. Someone must be thinking, "Yes, but what of the verse plays, *The Cocktail Party* and *J.B.* and others that have succeeded on Broadway?"

Show me a poetic drama that has a record run like *Oklahoma!* or *Abie's Irish Rose* (neither show *entirely* poetic!) and I'll concede the point.

ITEM (a statistical survey). Recently I have been invited into the homes of two former students, both of them English majors, both at least three years out of college, both in the teaching profession. After breakfast in the one case and high tea in the other, I poked around in my former students' libraries. From this authoritative sample of two former students I report, conclusively, that *my* former students now teaching English haven't bought a book of poetry, even a thirty-five-cent anthology of "best-loved poems," since graduation. Half of my sample, I add in despair, has either sold all the college texts he'd had to buy for his literature courses or (and I may be too optimistic) has them on his desk at school.

ITEM. A friend in publishing writes: "Collections of poems by a single poet are among the more prestigious trade books. We publish them largely for prestige. I don't think we've ever broken even on one."

Few publishers do. (What price prestige?) Ironically, since college curricula often support the luxury of courses dealing with poets and poetry, it is often economically sound to write on the interpretation of poetry or to edit anthologies. But unless one is a Robert Frost or an e. e. cummings, it is chancy to seek a livelihood by writing poetry. With anthologies proliferating and dominating the college scene, Academia seems to support the ward-workers but not the "unacknowledged legislators" of the race. My publishing friend says that college students buy those books professors tell them to buy. "Professors themselves usually get free desk copies!"

ITEM. From Josephine Miles, in the April 1963 issue of *The*

English Journal, published by the National Council of Teachers of English.

The general impression is that in America and England today there are almost infinite numbers of minor poets writing minor works and a few major poets writing major works, and almost nobody reading any of them. Certainly a number of facts bear out this assumption. In a country of millions, a reputable poet does well to sell 500 copies of a book, and these mostly to libraries. Books of poems rarely appear on bestseller lists, and when they do they are of not nearly so high a quality as most of the fiction appearing there.

ITEM. On January 24, 1966, President Johnson presented Congress with a budget calling for $5,300,000,000 for America's race into space. I received a letter dated January 26, 1966, from a former student, an English teacher for five years. "I know little things shouldn't matter so much," wrote my correspondent, "but I'm sick of all the little things that interfere with teaching. For two years I've asked for ten dollars to start a collection of paperback anthologies in my classroom. I've never gotten a single cent. If you could just *see* the equipment they buy for the chem lab. . . ."
With the blasting off into space of a menagerie of mice, monkeys, and men, poetry's thin hold on the edge of the literature curriculum was threatened. The reading and study of poetry in the classroom was almost lost in the roar of the rocket's thrust. In the months after the first Sputnik, no administrator-educator could take time to talk poetry. Our nation's schools were beefing up their programs in science and mathematics. (There was money for those programs.) If brave teachers of English said things about the humanities, they were understood to be talking about literacy or grammar or composition.
But now that some of our own chaps have orbited, bureaucracy has seen fit to include the study of English among those subject matters supported by tax monies. "Project English" grants and study centers are being funded by the public. The main business of "Project English" is the preparing and testing of classroom materials. In those centers where comprehensive curriculum programs are under way, poetry gets some attention. Among the reported individual and group proposals for research, however, there is seldom the hint that poetry exists and only a thin hint that literature is among the subject matters of English. Granted: "empirical" or "experimental" research is a tough, perhaps impossible business for

anyone venturing onto the thin ice of "feeling" or "appreciation" for art. But shouldn't researchers somewhere be lacing up their skates? Aren't data available, for example, concerning when student antagonism toward poetry begins to develop and what factors seem to cause this disaffection? Isn't whether narrative poems advantageously precede lyric poems in the curriculum a researchable question?

One more melancholy ITEM reflecting the feeble state of the art. My own survey of check-out records in the library of "a prominent liberal arts institution" discloses that five books of verse of prominent award-winning poets have remained inviolate in the stacks since purchase. A quote from the librarian of that institution: "Books of poetry are checked out in direct relation to the time and extent of assignments made by our English professors." This doleful comment led me to *The Humanities and the Library,* published by the American Library Association under the editorship of Lester Asheim.[3] "Despite these clichés about the ability of poetry to touch all men deeply," Asheim writes, "library experience would tend to show that the majority of average readers today are indifferent if not actually hostile to poetry, and that to many, poetry is considered to be an esoteric interest of literary aesthetes and not the common denominator of literary communication. . . . What little poetry does have an audience of any size is usually not the 'best' poetry by critical standards, and much of it is quite obviously doggerel by any standards." A public librarian offers corroboration. "I am becoming skittish about spending public funds for poetry," she writes. "Of course we should have some, but nobody looks at it."

I won't continue what might turn into a substantial documentation of the sad situation of the poet and of his art. Perhaps I put too much stress on the economics of the matter; poetry—in or out of the classroom—might well flourish (in some limited senses of the word) despite an accounting sheet that bleeds a history of financial peril.[4] Surely current scholarly and pedagogical journals give evi-

---

3. Chicago, 1957.
4. For some poets, at least, one of the happier fads is the "reading" sponsored by a college or university English department or a pro-Culture civic group. Although the poets most in demand for readings number only a dozen or two (and many of them hold sinecures in the professorial ranks), the scheduling of six or eight readings may bring a thousand dollars or so to the lucky poet. (What such activity costs the poet in poems is incalculable.) And if poet A appears on the campus of poet B, it is at least possible that poet B will sometime be tendered an invitation to read on A's campus. However, some of the "reading" poets are more irritated than pleased with the growing demand for public performance. "The people who show up to listen—to be entertained—seldom have any notion of the poet's work or even of poetry. They are there because some sympathetic host professor struck a bargain with his own classes: Show up for the reading and we won't hold class on Thursday." Thus complained one poet.

dence of a growing interest in the teaching of poetry—more interest at least than there was when Sputnik first voomed aloft.

All these items have been paraded to reinforce a single point. Here it is, again, unadorned: Teachers of English have failed as teachers of poetry. Even superior students dislike verse, by and large. If within the next generation we are to change the situation of poetry in the classroom, tomorrow's teacher will have to teach in ways different from today's.

Why teach poetry?

I ask this irreverent question so that I can attempt an answer. Of course, every teacher-to-be should frame his own answer before considering mine. A wide variety of reasons would seem to me plausible. Eschewing the grandiose, perhaps more important reasons for teaching poetry to the captives in our junior- and senior-high classes, I think at least three reasons merit some thought.

First, I teach poetry to students because poems, especially short poems, offer the unique opportunity of bringing complete works of art into focus. Short poems give a teacher a chance to perplex and persuade students into consideration of every word. Even the shortest short story, comparatively immense, resists such consideration. In this respect, a poem is more like a picture than a song: It is framed. It will stand still for study when study is called for; it will allow its parts to be added up into a total literary experience within the class period.

I don't know what, if anything, you'd want to ask or teach about this poem by Langston Hughes. I do think you would be able to engage most ninth-graders in whatever aspects of sound or meaning, whatever particulars of rhyme or image you chose to. You could surely ask students to compare the metaphors of the two stanzas. You could probably get them to consider with you the total performance.

Dreams

> Hold fast to dreams
> For if dreams die
> Life is a broken-winged bird
> That cannot fly.
>
> Hold fast to dreams
> For when dreams go
> Life is a barren field
> Frozen with snow.

A second reason for teaching poetry is that poetry tends to be richer, linguistically, than any other genre. Verse may help students see something of the possibilities of language. (If it were necessary to select only one device for "building broader vocabularies" or for "enriching sentence structure," I'd choose the study of poetry as the most promising.) I grant that the number of youngsters who become excited by the richness of language is limited; I'd bet that even more formidable are the odds against excitement from word study, prefix and suffix study, even from etymology and dictionary exercises, and surely from language workbooks.

Something, however, might happen to the literal-minded seventh-grader who is given a chance to read aloud or to hear and get with John Ciardi's:

> You see a new cow this way:
> A sod's-eye view of a munching dinosaur
> Peeling the grass from time,
> All sweetslobber and greenfleck
> In the going going going
> Of her machine jaws.

A tenth-grader, however modestly endowed, might catch R. P. Lister's playful personification the rising sun in "Winter Dawn":

> First he caught St. Mary's steeple,
>   Then he caught a dozen pubs;
> Then he caught the taller people,
>   And at last the smaller shrubs.

From repeated contact with such language, students may develop a sense of what language can do. Personal metaphor may begin to develop. Any such results will be more nourishing than those from Friday afternoon bouts with antonyms and synonyms or word histories.

Finally, I teach poetry simply because it *is* an exotic form. Students will seldom identify immediately with the "people" and the "situations" in poems. Good stories and plays tend to suck the reader into an emotional identification with character or situation; poems keep a prism of linguistic uniqueness between reader and experience. Prose tends to give readers conventional realities, however artistically arranged; poetry gives students enough perspective on reality that they can deal objectively with it.

Because the poet uses language uniquely, poems give young readers a chance to be objective about experience. Poets speak differently from the way young people speak; the young reader will not easily see himself in a poem. Consider the twelfth-grader who will ponder the kinds and levels of "discovery" in Keats' "On First Looking into Chapman's Homer": Keats' delight with discovery *might* emerge for the reader of the poem, but the "statement" of the poem wouldn't stand a chance as prose. For younger readers, even the lyric that speaks about life and death, love and honor, can sometimes get away with its subject matter.

There are higher sounding answers to this question—Why teach poetry? You might consider and debate the answers above. (I have another half-formed reason: When I teach poetry *successfully*, my students are given ammunition for their battles against conformity and faddism. Is there something there? Some adults say that adolescents are already amply armed for idiosyncrasy.)

I have argued three reasons why poetry should be taught: (1) poems let the teacher bring a complete work of art into focus, (2) poems are linguistically rich and therefore worth teaching; and (3) poems—exotic and prismatic—encourage consideration of life's realities. But a teacher's reasons for bringing poetry into class do not automatically provide directions for classroom practice. Translation is necessary: A teacher must discover "where" students are as to taste and capability, discover what they know and don't know about poetry; a teacher must make decisions as to what critical skills and what concepts, what poems and what poets he will teach in what order; he must settle on what approaches he will use in teaching different poems. Translating the rationale for poetry into classroom terms requires the setting of aims that reflect both the students' capabilities and the teacher's convictions about poetry.

Aims, general and specific

That a confusion of aims exists is apparent to anyone who visits classrooms in which poetry is being taught. Are teachers trying to "cover" the major American and English poets in the eleventh and twelfth grades? teach literary history rather than poetry? teach poems that will uplift their students? only entertain them? only instruct them?

Much bad teaching of poetry begins from concern for "covering" the anthology or the course of study. It proceeds in the desperate belief that there's reason for teaching early adolescents in the same way that *we* were taught, once we declared ourselves, at eighteen or twenty, to be majoring in English in college.

Too many high-school students "have" poetry by memorizing a little Shakespeare and a couple of couplets—pithy bits intended to serve them as *guideposts for living*. Too many students do no more than memorize poems, illustrate poems, scan poems, and report on poets' lives (the juicier elements already edited out by a wary encyclopedist). Too many students build short-lived glossaries of odd-sounding terms. They paraphrase. They underline similes, list ironies. They too often learn to dislike poetry. Overstatement, perhaps, but not grossly so.

We teach students to dislike poetry. The junior-high youngster who has not already turned away from the sissy stuff soon finds his native delight in the sound of poetry buried under an avalanche of technical terminology. We make it clear to our pupils that poetry is written about things that have no important place in their busy, anguished worlds: traveling Greeks, flowers, love songs, and birds, indeed! As the study of poetry progresses from elementary school to senior high school, it becomes increasingly an effeminate and esoteric subject matter; it becomes anathema to red-blooded adolescents. The activities we encourage and the results we get indicate confusion about aims. In cases where aims *are* clear, they are often unreasonable or unworthy. To reduce the prospect of confusion and to ensure that the teaching of poetry proceeds toward suitable goals, teachers must formulate aims that will lead students to an imaginative yet critical experience with poetry.

My most general aim in teaching poetry is to make it attractive enough that my pupils will become voluntary readers of poetry after they have escaped from my classes. Subsumed under this global hope are other general (but classroom-related) aims such as:

1. to provoke pleasure
2. to sharpen students' sense of observation
3. to improve students' taste in poetry
4. to increase students' skill in approaching poetry
5. to hint my own delight with poetry

It is reasonable that general aims for teaching poetry will sometimes remain a part of the teacher's mystique. But when it comes to considering specific teaching aims, which general aims must eventually become, the mystique is no longer defensible. Specific aims affect the classroom lives of students directly; students deserve to know where each lesson is going; and they will often contribute usefully to the shaping (and the reaching) of specific teaching aims.

My *specific* aim in teaching a poem varies with each poem. Through particular poems, I might show how a dramatic monolog works or what metaphor means or how sound systems work. I might try to demonstrate a poet's obsession with the sensuous through one poem, show something about poetic diction through another. My specific aim is relevant to—and limited by—the poem I'm trying to teach.

Might specific aims, if realized, encourage my students to become *voluntary* readers of poetry? I mean something as simple here as the reading of the verse tucked away in the corners of popular magazines. The answer is Yes, *if* specific aims are limited in number and developed concretely, *if* aims are intellectually honest and developed through stimulating poems.

Vague, trivial, or pedestrian aims have not been the sole villains responsible for our conspicuous lack of success in teaching poetry: The easy excitements of the mass media, the private and impenetrable poems of some poets, and the wary exclusion of "touchy" poems by some anthologists contribute to the "Why do we hafta study the stuff?" queries. But more to the point is the fact that the principles we follow in the future must be different from those we have followed in the past.

Some principles for teaching poetry

From observations in junior- and senior-high classrooms, I sometimes conclude that what is being taught about poetry is only that mysterious difference in stress between iamb and trochee or the particular ways in which the Shakespearean sonnet differs from the Petrarchan. I see pupils taking frantic notes in the belief that poetry will finally reveal itself and grow beautiful—once a certain succession of Tudor monarchs is mastered. I conclude that teachers, beginning with the junior-high grades, teach the things that will prepare students for a particular college-entrance exam (last administered *circa* 1936).

What I see and sense, in short, persuades me that the general goal of making their pupils voluntary readers of poetry has not seemed to enough teachers a reasonable or worthy aim. Were this goal suddenly to assume reasonableness and worthiness, a drastic change in teaching method would be needed to achieve it. It is the aim of making readers of poetry that prompts the following prin-

ciples. The first two principles focus more on the teacher than on
teaching or on the pupil.

  *Principle one: The teacher who is not himself a reader of poetry
must not pretend to teach poetry.* I mean this bald dictum to be
taken quite literally. Many teachers who now teach poetry should
stop—unless they can be persuaded to find time for poetry in
their own reading lives. Students, teachers, the literature curriculum, poets, poetry, and society would be better off were this principle effectively legislated. Taken literally, this principle would mean
that some students would proceed through the junior- and senior-
high grades without instruction in reading or interpreting poetry. It
would imply a chaos of different backgrounds among students
leaving or graduating from high school; it would mean a compounding of the lack of sequence or structure of the nation's high-
school literature programs; it would mean that the literature curriculum would get even more public abuse than it now enjoys. I would
risk these things.

  For most teachers of English, poetry is mica, not bedrock:
Grammar and composition, the bulkier genres of drama and prose
seem to them probably more important and surely more significant.
Teachers continue after their college careers to read novels, personal
narrative, other nonfiction, and—less often—drama; few read poetry.
That they don't themselves read poetry, voluntarily, is due in part
to the instruction they received in college literature courses. There,
future teachers learned that poetry was something to be thoroughly
dissected and consummately respected rather than read all-of-a-
piece and enjoyed. Dazzling professorial explications substituted
for their own close reading.

  If indeed many teachers of English read poetry only when
required for an annual rehearsal of lesson plans, what must happen
to poetry in the classroom? To consider this is to quake. Might not
many of the unfortunate reactions that youngsters demonstrate be
explained by the fact that teachers of English are not readers of
poetry?

  No legislature will decree that teachers who don't read poetry
must not teach it. Indeed, simply managing somehow to have
teachers *read* poetry would guarantee no particular teaching success.
But I labor this idea because of what happens in the classroom.
How can the teacher who doesn't read poetry build interest in it
from his own indifference? Isn't bad teaching inevitable from such a
teacher? Will he not retreat to the explications, the biographies, the
histories, and the matters of form and versification that he finds in

his text or revives from his college notes? Will not the nonreader accept whatever poems are readily available to him? Are not these the disorders that must characterize teaching by the nonreader of poetry?

The point is not to condemn. There's nothing worse in not being a reader of poetry than there is in not being up on one of the new grammars. But since poetry *is* a special case, fighting for life in the battle of curriculum survival, I would prefer that it be left out of the curriculum altogether than be taught by teachers who do not read it.

At the same time, I would exhort teachers of English to read the verse that appears in the magazines they read, to browse in whatever libraries are available, to buy some verse—and to do these things with an eye to the relevance of their reading to their own classrooms. This exhortation leads, I think, to a second principle.

Principle two: The teacher of poetry must teach only those poems for which he can engender real enthusiasm. This strikes me as an attractive proposition. More will "happen" in the classroom of the teacher who is enthusiastic about what he is doing. That hard-to-pin-down quality of *appreciation* will not materialize in the classroom of the teacher bored silly with poem X. Might each reader be persuaded to raise his hand and pledge, with some solemnity, "I shall never teach a poem I don't genuinely like"?

Translated literally, this principle means that the teacher who truly likes Robert Service and doesn't care much for Edgar Allan Poe will teach Service and bypass Poe. What will happen to the great poems? The great traditions? How can we ensure the student's contact with the very best poems in the heritage? What will become of Milton and Yeats?

The easy answer to these questions is that the great poems, the great traditions, and the great poets will survive despite what does or does not happen in our classrooms. (A handful of students will find their ways to the pure stuff even if it's kept under lock and key!) A better answer is that there are in most schools teachers of broad, comprehensive taste; chances are good that students will sometimes be in contact with such teachers. The best answer may be that teachers who are—or will become—readers of poetry will broaden and improve their taste and teaching as they read.

And if they don't? What of the students in Nowhereville High who suffer four years in the classroom of Nowhereville's one and only English teacher? And that teacher thinks that Eddie Guest is all there is to poetry?

So be it! Better Eddie Guest taught enthusiastically than Housman taught wretchedly. At the *very worst*, in the class of the Guest enthusiast, students will be exposed to reams of second-rate verse. But there the ultimate disservice will not be done: the Guest aficionado will not generate so active a distaste for poetry that all other teachers will be kept forever from persuading students that there is something to poetry, after all.

Since few of the poems any one teacher really likes will be available in a given anthology, there are other implications. The course of study and the text will sometimes be ignored. The teacher will feature chalkboard and (with an eye on current copyright law) the mimeograph machine. He will sometimes cut a poem from a magazine or tear up a paperback. He will often read aloud. The poetry curriculum will become an expression of the teacher's own taste. The *responsible* teacher will seek to become more catholic in his reading.

The responsible teacher will assess his own blind spots and attempt to bring light to the dark corners of his mind. If the poetry of the Beats speaks most clearly to him, he will try to make Whitman and Dickinson come alive; if predisposed toward Pope, he will try to discover what it is about Yeats or Dylan Thomas that so excites some readers.

The teacher who does not respond to poetry can observe Principle Two by bringing into his classroom someone who reads it well; he can give students the chance to collect candidates for this year's version of the "our favorite poems" collection.

One college teacher of English took sharp issue with this principle. "Enthusiasm is important," he agreed, "but student exposure to the very finest poetry is even more important. The anthologies are reliable if unexciting guides here." He argued from his own experiences as a college teacher. A substantial piece of Milton's *Paradise Lost* was in the text used for the sophomore survey. An anti-Milton or indifferent-to-Milton man at the outset, he had to come to know the anthologized selection intimately in order to teach it. Intimacy, in this case, bred love rather than contempt. His own appreciation for Milton developed slowly but steadily over his eight years' tenure as a college professor.

But I wonder how many of his students from those first six years in the soph survey are reading Milton today.

I hold with the principle. Teach those poems that excite you. Circumvent those anthology selections that bore you, are beyond you, or beneath you. If confronted with a course of study studded with poems you cannot—or will not—handle, use the dodge of the record player, the feint of the "read this for tomorrow" assignment, or the subterfuge of an oral reading carefully prepared by a dependable pupil.

Irresponsible? Consider again some earlier points. Not all teachers of English are readers of poetry. This fact is a basic reason for our failure. One wouldn't insist that high-school teachers of English be forced to prove themselves readers of poetry in order to keep their jobs. But one might insist that the individual who is not a reader of poetry be jailed for letting his own indifference to poetry breed indifference in his students. I think the nonreader-teacher of poetry inevitably produces nonreader-students.

Let those teachers of English whose dish is not poetry do well what they can do. Let them emphasize grammar or language principles, develop creative dramatics programs; let them help youngsters learn composition strategies or understand the mass media. Let them do well whatever it was that attracted them to the teaching of English. Youngsters will survive and poetry will survive despite its exclusion from any one teacher's classes. And we've already seen that there are circumventions — letting the student who likes poetry read some poems, bringing the record player or the local poet into the classroom.

The following four principles relate more directly to teaching.

Principle three: The teacher must keep experience with poetry itself at the center of his teaching. Too often we let the study of biography, of philology, of intellectual and cultural milieu, or, more often, of versification substitute for the reading of poetry, substitute for experience with poetry. In many classrooms the study of poetry consists of twice as much data concerning the backgrounds of poems as is either useful or enlightening. Each year there are thousands of students graduating from our high schools who know glib generalizations about Romanticism and precise facts about Poe's private life but who have never *experienced* a poem by either Keats or Poe.

Somehow we lead youngsters to believe that poems are largely autobiographical. We need to teach them or, better, to show them that poets are not under oath to reveal their innermost selves, to speak from conviction, to say what they believe. Sometimes they do; but sometimes they speak with other voices. Of course literary history has its fascinating aspects. Of course some poems will be illuminated by biography. Knowing something of Milton's life speaks to the reading of "On His Blindness." But excesses are the issue.

I think the excesses might be proved. The proving apparatus involves a random sample of last year's graduates who are willing to have anodes — or some such device — taped to their skulls, a stimulus-machine feeding the anodes, and a marvelously sensitive response-recorder attached — where? To the students' hearts? (Some details remain to be worked out.) But into the apparatus I feed a set of stimuli. From it I get a neatly typed translation of the students' immediate responses.

What would happen? Stimulus Number 1, William Shakespeare. Number 2, Oscar Wilde. Number 3, Edgar Allan Poe. Number 4, John Keats.

What responses would emerge? For Shakespeare, "Ann Hathaway," "Stratford," or an imperfectly remembered line from Brutus or Hamlet. For Wilde, a garbled thought about some jail, somewhere. For Poe, "Took dope" or "Nevermore." For Keats, "Died at an early age."

Died at an early age! True. Interesting, even, in a melancholy way. But is this poetry? Might such responses actually occur? If they might, is this what students should remember about poetry? Mightn't we hope instead for an image that can't be forgotten, a sound that still echoes, an idea that still reverberates?

In arguing for teaching "the poem *itself*" rather than "*about* the poem," Elizabeth Rose says that such things as these can be taught: that poems can be about anything; that they can be written for different purposes and are written in different forms (to "tell a rather long story or sing a short little song"); "that a poem has a slightly different meaning for everyone who reads it"; that some poems rhyme but others don't; that poems use words that "make the reader see things vividly, hear things clearly, smell things keenly, feel things sharply"; that poems often use figurative comparisons; and that poems have rhythm.[5]

Those, I think, are things *about* poetry that *are* profitably taught through the study of poems. But we are so often busy with Byron's love life or Pound's fascism that our students never experience both ugly poems and pretty poems, poems that delight and others that frighten. They don't learn that some poems swing and others don't; that the language of poetry tends to be different from other language (in ways such as compactness and word order); that poets often pun and juxtapose unlikely things, often speak ironically, and often use ambiguity deliberately rather than accidentally.

As matters stand, we teach things about poetry that can't pos-

---

5. "Teaching Poetry in the Junior High School," *The English Journal,* XLVI, Dec. 1957, pp. 540–550.

sibly come out of the reading of a poem. As we indulge in history and background, biography and verse form, such things as what poems do are ignored.

Norman Nathan's *Judging Poetry*[6] has an epigraph on the cover, "Some judge of authors' names, not works, and then / Nor praise nor blame the writing, but the men."[7] Nathan asks the student: "Can you judge poetry? Or are you one of those who become enthusiastic if Shakespeare wrote it and look askance if that prolific writer, Anonymous, was the author? Are you impressed by big names? by tornado-like critics? by standards of value?" Or, I might add, is your sense of excellence influenced too greatly by your own teachers' judgments?

Following I. A. Richards in his revealing *Practical Criticism*,[8] Nathan suggests the necessity for separating the poem from the poet and his milieu—if helping students judge and truly enjoy poetry is what we teachers are after. We need to take into the classroom, more often then we have, poems unidentified as to author and time or tradition and let the poem speak for itself.

Consider the following poem. If it is a poem you think just right for a class of self-consciously mature tenth-graders, or too graphic a scene of watermelon-eating to be kept from an eighth-grade class working away on vivid detail in written descriptions, it should be a part of your poetry curriculum. And questions of the poem's meaning and quality and technique could *be* questions rather than facts.

Reflections on a Gift of Watermelon Pickle
Received from a Friend called Felicity

> During that summer
> When unicorns were still possible;
> When the purpose of knees
> Was to be skinned;
> When shiny horse chestnuts
> (Hollowed out
> Fitted with straws
> Crammed with tobacco
> Stolen from butts
> In family ashtrays)
> Were puffed in green lizard silence

6. New York: G. P. Putnam's Sons, 1961.
7. From Alexander Pope, *Essay on Criticism*, Part II.
8. New York: Harcourt, Brace & Co., 1929.

While straddling thick branches
Far above and away
From the softening effects
Of civilization;

During that summer—
Which may never have been at all;
But which has become more real
Than the one that was—
Watermelons ruled.

Thick pink imperial slices
Melting frigidly on sun-parched tongues
Dribbling from chins;
Leaving the best part,
The black bullet seeds,
To be spit out in rapid fire
Against the wall
Against the wind
Against each other;

And when the ammunition was spent,
There was always another bite:
It was a summer of limitless bites,
Of hungers quickly felt
And quickly forgotten
With the next careless gorging.

The bites are fewer now.
Each one is savored lingeringly,
Swallowed reluctantly.

But in a jar put up by Felicity,
The summer which maybe never was
Has been captured and preserved.
And when we unscrew the lid
And slice off a piece
And let it linger on our tongue:
Unicorns become possible again.

                                   JOHN TOBIAS

Since he is not well known, Tobias' life, his critical convictions, and his leisure-time pursuits would necessarily go unremarked in most teachers' classes. Would the poem thus be better or less well taught?

Principle four: The teacher must teach the mechanics of poetry inductively. By *mechanics* here I mean such diverse things as versification—meter and rhyme—and the special vocabulary of poetry—such as caesura, metaphor, and symbol. Teachers must stop first defining these things and then sending students off on a scavenger hunt to find examples of them. By *inductive* I mean that the reaching of generalizations about poetry comes after repeated experience with examples that lead to those generalizations.

The laws of learning are ignored by the teacher who begins teaching poetry through a rehearsal of iamb and trochee. Teaching such aspects of poetry in isolation from the reading of poetry is akin to studying verbals in isolation from student writing. Neither works. The laws of learning suggest that learning occurs best in context. Facts about poetry, labels for certain phenomena, are best remembered or learned when they come out of the material they concern. The complicated matter of rhythm in poetry might some-day be learned by students helped to feel and see and consider the rhythms in poems they read; it will not be learned in any useful way outside the context of reading poetry. Even a beginning sense of metaphor needs to be developed through examination of meta-phors that succeed (and others that fail) in a variety of poems; this sense will not grow out of a week's work on definition of the terms of versification.

Learning occurs best when its sequence is from simple to complex. Students can readily learn to define the narrative poem as one that "tells a story," but such easy definition doesn't help them read narrative poems better. Understanding specific narrative strategies and their effects is more instructive. For example, some stanzas of Carryl's rollicking "Robinson Crusoe" could be inter-changed without injuring the poem's relatively loose structure. A look at "Robinson Crusoe" would usefully come before considera-tion of poems with tighter, more complex narrative structures. Benét's "Jesse James" adds the minor complication of refrain, for example, and has within it groups of stanzas whose sequence is inevitable rather than random. Still more subtle are the structures of Noyes' "The Highwayman," James Weldon Johnson's "The Crea-tion," and De la Mare's "The Listeners." Each poem has a unique narrative technique. How (and how effectively) each works is the important consideration. Surely primitive narrative techniques must be carefully considered before subtler narrative devices (such as Browning's in "My Last Duchess") can be taught meaningfully. Before definition is useful, students must have read, read aloud, listened to, and understood *particular* strategies.

In teaching students who know nothing about metaphor, I might begin with the metaphor they use and hear—theirs, "You're losing your marbles," or mine, "That excuse is hard to swallow"—and move toward popular songs. I might avoid "You Ain't Nothin' But a Hound Dog" only because it is, happily, a thing of the past. "Love Is a Many-Splendored Thing" is old but perfectly suitable. The metaphor of speech and song, then, before the tougher, tighter metaphor of most poetry. I would move this slowly from simple to complex in any grade where metaphor needed to be taught. Indeed, the principle of simple to complex would hold even in the senior year, were metaphor still a mystery there. I would go back to the beginnings: Twelfth-graders who cannot make metaphor operational when they read probably have a lot of funny notions about what it is.

The things we teach about poetry—the terms, the tricks, the techniques—need to be taught as poetry is read, not taught in isolation from it. This doesn't mean that one teaches only those things that come to mind casually as he is discussing a poem. Instead, poems are chosen for teaching in part because a point about poetry can be made from them. For example, John Ciardi sometimes talks about the *fulcrum* in a poem—the point of balance, the place in a poem where a key word or image somehow separates what has gone before from what is to come. The verb *committed* may mark such a point in this poem by Louis Simpson.

The Heroes

I dreamed of war-heroes, of wounded war-heroes
With just enough of their charms shot away
To make them more handsome. The women moved nearer
To touch their brave wounds and their hair streaked with gray.

I saw them in long ranks ascending the gang-planks;
The girls with the doughnuts were cheerful and gay.
They minded their manners and muttered their thanks;
The Chaplain advised them to watch and to pray.

They shipped these rapscallions, these sea-sick battalions
To a patriotic and picturesque spot;
They gave them new bibles and marksmen's medallions,
Compasses, maps, and committed the lot.

A fine dust has settled on all that scrap metal.
The heroes were packaged and sent home in parts

To pluck at a poppy and sew on a petal
And count the long night by the stroke of their hearts.

How many meanings might *committed* have? Certainly *committed* works on a first level as a term of military strategy: a general commits troops to a particular action or battle zone. Just as surely, but less obviously, *committed* anticipates the institution to which the packaged heroes were sent: we commit people to insane asylums and to veterans' hospitals. There may be other senses of *committed* at work. The poem hints that the "rapscallions" lack personal commitment: they are pawns in a horrible game.

The reader who senses *committed* to be a point of fulcrum reads the last stanza differently from the first three. The last stanza must be read soberly; the first three are almost gay and comically ironic; they are filled with funny words and almost funny images; "just enough of their charms shot away / To make them more handsome"; "rapscallions, these sea-sick battalions" are given "new bibles and marksmen's medallions." These won't protect them.

"The Heroes" might be taught because it provides good opportunity for considering how fulcrum works. The idea of fulcrum might be the basis for reading and studying the poem in class. But the method of study would be inductive. Oral readings by students will produce a noticeable change in tone of voice when the final stanza is read. "Why does this happen?" you might ask. One student might notice the shift from simple past to present perfect. Another notices the stern harshness of the images in the final stanza as contrasted with the images of the first three. And then: "At what particular point, with what *word*, is the shift from light to serious signaled?" If you can get this far, you can say something about (and illustrate on the chalkboard) a balance point, a fulcrum.

Perhaps entirely different things might be taught from "The Heroes." For example, the abstract subjects of versification might be made concrete and interesting: the anapests, except for conventional substitutions, are maintained throughout; they shift most significantly with a beginning stress in the tone-changing twelfth line. There are the end rhymes and (in almost every line) the inner rhymes and chimes. Assonance and alliteration might be considered. Some interesting teaching might cover the ambiguities (including uncertain pronouns and the complicated time sequence) and the ironies (the missing charms, the *brave* wounds, the soldiers' equipage, *et al.*). *Particular* points must be made as poems are taught. Only rarely will a class be ready to consider all points that *might* be made.

Wouldn't such teaching take forever? (It will sometimes seem so.) Isn't there danger that students will be indifferent to or not get to the point the teacher has in mind? (Yes. But there are ways.) Won't there sometimes be no reaction at all? Isn't it easier just to tell students what it is in a poem you want them to see? (True, true. But if you are asking questions well enough and leading students wisely enough and have firmly enough in mind a point worth making, chances are good that students will be engaged in what it is you're about. Once engaged, they might learn. Perhaps they will learn what you hoped they would.)

One question more: Isn't it hard to cover the subject matter of poetry this way? (Not just hard. Impossible. But so is every other way impossible. If you choose a poem with a particular class in mind and get ready to go as far with that poem as student response and interest allow you to go, some learning will occur. More important, perhaps, the students' ability to look hard at a poem will become more important than your own capabilities as explicator of texts. This seems relevant to the issue of teaching.)

Let me conclude this point through reference to the first two verses of another war poem, Henry Reed's "Naming of Parts." What I would hope to teach in this poem is that there is sometimes more than one voice "speaking" in a poem. Sometimes, as if to compound the problems of the unskilled reader of poetry, the poet "forgets" to offer such helps as new paragraphs or quotation marks to mark his separate voices. Yet surely, in the stanzas below, students can be helped to hear two voices.

Today we have naming of parts. Yesterday,
We had daily cleaning. And tomorrow morning,
We shall have what to do after firing. But today,
Today we have naming of parts. Japonica
Glistens like coral in all of the neighbouring gardens,
    And today we have naming of parts.

This is the lower sling swivel. And this
Is the upper sling swivel, whose use you will see,
When you are given your slings. And this is the piling swivel,
Which in your case you have not got. The branches
Hold in the gardens their silent, eloquent gestures,
    Which in our case we have not got.

"What seems to be going on?" you ask. "What are the *parts* part of? Where is this lesson taking place? Is it wartime or peace? What people seem to be present in the poem? What people talk? Is there more than one voice? Are you sure? Where in each stanza does that second voice begin talking? Can you point to any pronouns in the second stanza that support the idea of two voices? [you-your, we-our] How about the first stanza, again? One speaker or two *there?*" Once the dust settles after this debate, you can go on to ask what the two voices are like and how they—or the speakers—differ.

This, I think, would be an engaging, stimulating twenty minutes. If the poem didn't work at all (and you'd know this within a very few minutes), it would be shoved back in your "Poems" folder for another day with another class. But if it worked, something of value about poetry would be learned by some students. If it worked, students would have had one more experience with poetry that would equip them for the next, more complicated confrontation.

Principle five: Teachers must stop overexplaining poems. Great are the temptations of detailed explication; few are its benefits—if the explanations and interpretations are exclusively the teacher's. In extreme cases, overexplication terminates with the poetry exam on which pupils are expected to come up with the "right" paraphrases. The right paraphrases, of course, are those laid out by the teacher during "discussion."

Although the teacher surely has the responsibility to be fully ready to speculate about and to suggest interpretations for the poems he chooses to teach, the teaching issue is whether the student can be persuaded into a consideration of a poem and encouraged to try his own explications. "What might this mean?" is a better question than "What does this mean?" "For what reasons might the poet . . . ?" is a better beginning to involvement than an imperious "What Edgar Lee Masters obviously has in mind, here, . . ."

Students must be encouraged to develop and state their own ideas about possible meanings in poetry. When what they think about meaning is off the continuum of possibility and reasonableness, a useful teacher response might be a candid, "I don't think you can defend that from the poem. Can you?" Considerable class time must go into debate among students concerning possible interpretations. The teacher's role is the challenging of the unsupportable, the genial refutation of the foolish, and the delighted support of all thoughtful response.

Only willful or ignorant misinterpretation is to be *corrected.* Although I. A. Richards has demonstrated how little we teachers know about poetry (once the names of the poets and the milieu from which the poems come are denied us), we can confidently explain to Charlie, "No, Sandburg doesn't mean Australia there in 'Grass.' It's Austerlitz, Charlie. Austerlitz, you see, is the name of a town. . . ." We can stop Josie halfway through her explication of Auden's "Musée des Beaux Arts" when it becomes clear that she confuses Icarus with Apollo.

Poems are patently susceptible to more than one interpretation. I believe that the best interpretation is my own; I have the inescapable responsibility for working toward that interpretation as I prepare to teach a particular poem. But when I'm teaching well, I remember that a student who is frequently "wrong" in his interpretations will not easily essay again if I respond to his answers with ridicule. Again, involving students in the consideration of a poem is far more important than trying to teach theme exactly as I happen to see it. Some poems we "teach," therefore, should be those that defy elaborate explications and yet allow considerable discussion.

If I were to teach H. J. Gottleib's "Angler's Choice" to a class of eighth-graders, I'd first put the poem on the board.

> These he cast
> Where the pool lay still
> Under a lichened ledge:
> Silver Doctor, Olive Quill,
> Ibis, Lady Beaverkill
>   And a Dark Blue Sedge.

> These he chose
> For the stony flat
> Spanned by the covered bridge:
> Royal Coachman, Cahill, Gnat,
> March Brown, Little Marryat,
>   And a Berry Midge.

> These he tried
> In the fading light
> Down by the alder thicket:
> Yellow Sally, Sandy Mite,
> Wickham's Fancy, Cocky Knight,
>   And a real, live cricket.

Next I'd read it aloud and then have the students read it aloud with me. I'd ask about the proper nouns: "Has anyone a guess about what all these capitalized nouns might be?" If there weren't even an uncertain guess, I'd answer my question. If someone asked what *lichened* meant, I'd explain. If interest were there in the students' faces, I might try a question about the poem's sequence or order: "Might the first two stanzas be reversed? Might the third stanza come first? Why not?"

If the fact that there's a fisherman fishing can be made clear, little else need be. Either the sound of the poem delights or the reader is indifferent to it. *Perhaps* Gottleib has in mind some metaphysical network of relationship among the various flies. *Perhaps* that "real, live cricket" implies the rejection of the mechanical and the embracing of the natural. But I wouldn't bet on either possibility. Neither would I look for a student to put on a fly-tying demonstration as preparation for my class's reading of the poem.

Overexplication is one curse of the poetry-reading class.

Principle six: The poetry unit must give way to the occasional teaching of poetry. I recently observed one day in the fourth week of a carefully planned four-week unit on lyric poetry. The teacher was animated and skillful; the poems were well chosen for this tenth-grade honors section; the students were bored silly. During another visit to an eleventh-grade classroom in a state that hadn't seen a lasting snow for over a decade, I learned from a student that the class was just finishing a three-week unit on "Snowbound." Moving from the particular isolation of "Snowbound" to the universal experience might have worked. But this particular teacher contented herself with "providing vicarious experience in depth." The depth was there, all right, as she examined each swirling flake in Whittier's poem. She made a travesty both of "depth" and of "vicarious experience." Students learned to loathe snow, not to feel it.

The intense nature of poetry demands that it be taught sparingly, that it be used to season the other subject matters of the English class. Poetry is too rich and too demanding for sustained units. And not only are there things wrong with the sustained unit, there are attractive things about the occasional teaching of poetry. A poem or two studied meaningfully complement the study of a short story. (In Jennings and Calitri's *Stories*[9] many stories are paired with poems. The first pair puts Saroyan's "Romance" with Edna St. Vincent Millay's "Recuerdo," and another ties together a Ray Bradbury story and an Emily Dickinson poem.) Surely some

9. Frank G. Jennings and Charles J. Calitri, *Stories* (New York: Harcourt, Brace & Co., 1957).

good must come out of the natural joining of different literary types when the two illuminate each other.

Sometimes the unit—pared down to a class hour or two—will consist of poems of a particular kind or tradition or subject. The fog-is-cat metaphor in Sandburg's omnipresent "Fog" is considered along with Melville Cane's "Fog, the Magician" and with T. S. Eliot's eight lines beginning "The yellow fog that rubs its back upon the window-panes" from "Prufrock." Four or five *carpe diem* poems are selected from that tradition begun by the ancients and continuing in the present; how various poets use or view similar subjects is a basis for grouping poems together—a set of crow poems (see those by Gustave Keyser, Judson Jerome, and Leah Drake on pages 80 and 84) or a set of car poems (see those by Edith May Alcock, May Swenson, and Laurence Lieberman on pages 82 and 89). Poems in a set need to have just enough in common to allow their being grouped. Teachers who read poetry with an eye to what poems will fit their classes and "speak" to each other will find useful sets galore.

Teaching poetry occasionally or incidentally needn't mean teaching it casually or indifferently. In setting the unit aside and replacing it with a series of shorter, cutting-across-time-and-type lessons, the teacher makes poetry a much more natural part of the classroom. (Does anything pleasant ever happen after the announcement, "Now we're going to begin our unit on poetry"?) Poetry is taught in relation to other literature. It sometimes comes into the composition process as model. It is read aloud by students who are prepared for its reading. An appropriate poem is read when the day is gloomy, when students are restless, or when the air is tight with the excitement of a momentous current event. It is used during that final fifteen minutes of the class hour as a substitute for the desperate announcement, "Get out your books now and study." Yet it is not taught without plan or purpose.

The teacher willing to enrich his class through the reading and studying of poems will have a folder of poems that lend themselves to those fifteen-minute voids squeezed between pep assemblies and early lunch periods. He will have a folder of poems that he thinks will "go" with his students, poems susceptible to their understanding, poems that speak of interesting subjects, poems for which he himself "has engendered an enthusiasm." Many poems will simply be read aloud once or twice. Then a moment of questioning silence. And then, should nothing be happening—lifted eyebrows or quizzical grimaces—the poems are slipped back into the teacher's folder for presentation another time. There's value to students in simply hearing a poem read well; they need much experience simply hearing poems. It is no violation of professional ethics to suggest that the teacher go beyond the course of study, clip some poems he likes, and read them at times which seem to him appropriate

The classroom might thus be a congenial, friendly place wherein students and teachers sometimes read verse. A poem is a life-saving oasis in the desert of nonrestrictive clauses and S-V-O's. Many times students will talk about the poem they've read; often they will write about it. Moreover, the teacher's folder will have in it poems that give him a basis for teaching important things about the reading of poetry. As he himself progresses as a reader, the teacher finds poems that group themselves together and provide proper material for teaching those things he knows need to be taught.

In one of the very best moments in my own teaching life, the incidental approach to poetry provided this opportunity.

I had Robert Francis' poem "Pitcher" in a folder among some thirty poems. (The poem is given on page 40.) One springtime day I arrived at my classroom, anticipating a first-period session with tenth-graders, only to find a classroom window broken and a telltale baseball lying with broken glass and putty on the floor. The guilty student, a member of that first-period class, came to class early to explain what had happened. During baseball practice Danny had tipped a foul high enough that it eluded the backstop, bounced once on a cement walk, and subsequently made illegal entry into my classroom. We cleaned up the mess. I told Danny he could keep the baseball even though he offered it to me. I gave him a copy of "Pitcher."

At the end of the class period the following day, we had ten minutes. Danny was ready. He read the poem and, from his starting pitcher's perspective, explicated some of it. The girls learned everything about baseball they wanted to know.

But my moment came the following week. The baseball team was having its first practice game. I stopped to watch an inning or two. Our boys were at bat when I got there. And Danny on his knees in front of the batter's bench for the home team was explaining it all: "'The others throw to be comprehended,' you guys," he said, quoting from the poem. "Get it?"

The three principles following focus more on the student than on the teacher.

Principle seven: Students must often have the chance to choose what poetry they will read, study, and discuss. We know pretty well who decides what poems students will study. The bookmakers and the curriculum-makers — legitimately, if by default — dictate the poetry curriculum. One editor (properly sensitive to the charge that publishers perpetuate the poetry curriculum) redirects the blame at the classroom teacher. "The bookmaster who gets out of line," he writes, "is likely to lose his shirt." Publishers spend more money than many school systems trying to find out what innovation they can get away with. They conclude: Not much. Any publisher who passes up a "canonized" piece — "The Rime of the Ancient Mariner" or a substantial section from "Idylls of the King" — may lose a text adoption because of such omission.

There is, then, little enough experimentation and innovation in the popular literature anthologies. Instead of throwing the anthology away, as some have argued, we should be thankful for the many good selections in anthologies and select and choose from them. But at the same time, teachers must feel free to bring in, and have students bring in, more and fresher poems than publishers feel they can afford.

There are many areas of the curriculum about which students have no right to voice their preferences. No tenth-grade student should be allowed to avoid certain important composition jobs simply because he sees no immediate pleasure or profit in them. But since poetry, unlike composition, is struggling to stay alive in the curriculum, students might be given repeated opportunities to ferret out and bring into the classroom poems which seem to speak clearly and interestingly to them.

There are awesome implications. Some students may be counted on to bring in wretched verse. But if the poems that students find for class study actually represent their own responses to poetry, if the classroom is honestly a place where taste is an issue and not a predetermined fact, the teacher will begin with the cheap, sentimental poem and ask questions; he will look with students at a diseased figure and seek improvements and comment; he will ask whether a rhyme dictated by form is less than perfection itself. When possible, the teacher will put the poor poem up against one a little bit finer. Better, perhaps, he will challenge a student to do so.

Poems selected by students, examined and questioned critically but impersonally, will put some of the burden for selecting, reading, and explicating onto the student. This is where the burden belongs.

Following the principle will mean that a lot of second-rate verse is brought into the class. It will mean devoting class time to Charlie's hand-picked poem, "Try Smiling," which begins:

When the weather suits you not, try smiling.
When your coffee isn't hot, try smiling.
When your neighbors don't do right or your relatives all fight,
Sure 'tis hard, but then you might try smiling.

Charlie may think that that's a fine poem; he has that right. The
teacher has the responsibility, however, to ask questions enough to
provoke Charlie into questioning his own satisfaction; Charlie must
not be forever content with the poem. The teacher will help the
student smoke out the easy sentiments. Charlie can be helped to see
that smiling like an idiot despite such unrelated calamities as cool
coffee and fighting kinfolk will achieve nothing more than his
candidacy for the insane asylum.

So we ask: "What advice does the poem give? Is it good advice? Does smiling about cool coffee seem just as important as
smiling when neighbors 'don't do right'? What might 'don't do
right' mean? Are there times when 'just smiling' is about all you can
do? Can you think of times when something else might be better?"

Such talk about the poem's didactic might just barely qualify as
talk about poetry. Nothing was said about verse form, language, or
symbol; nothing was noted about the poet's life or about the tradition ("The Poet's Corner" in the *Weekly News?*) from which the
poem prematurely sprang. Something might have happened, however, to Charlie's taste.

Witness. Encouraged by—and interested in—all the discussion
that "Try Smiling" provided, Charlie later brings in another "smile"
poem:

Let others cheer the winning man,
There's one I hold worthwhile.
'Tis he who does the best he can,
Then loses with a smile.

Beaten he is, but not to stay
Down with the rank and file;
That man will win another day,
Who loses with a smile.

Charlie's taste, you say, hasn't developed much. (Developing taste
takes time.) But at least you can pretend that "win" here might
imply winning in some larger way before you start in to generate
dissatisfaction with form and idea.

Perhaps the job of the English teacher is to improve student
taste in poetry rather than attempt to dictate it. If so, this implies

starting where students are in their tastes and interests. (If you think unwarranted my assumptions about where Charlie and his classmates often are as to taste, sometime arrange to have your students express their preferences from among four or five poems you put in front of them—one or two poems you think are true poetic performances, the others—larded with advice, puppies, grandmothers, and old swimming holes—you know are slapdash versifying. Be of strong heart as you examine the results of the preference poll.) Starting where students are, with an eye to moving them forward, implies giving students the responsibility for choosing much of the poetry to be studied. You'll have the chance to demonstrate your own taste through the poems you choose to bring in.

Principle eight: Students who are asked to read and study poetry must sometimes be asked to say something poetically. Of course students will say poetic things without being asked. But I suggest here the providing of assignments and exercises *requiring* the conscious effort to say something as well as it can be said.

A student's serious effort to reduce a good idea to better expression may create an alliance (or a peace treaty, at least) between student and poem. I'm extending the idea of the sympathetic compact. Once students know how extremely difficult it is to get "the right words in the right order," they may be interested in judging the rightness of the poet's order. Other activities, choral reading or a recording, are prominent among explicit methods promoting "appreciation." But involving students in the effort to order something into poetry or into something poetic stands first among my recommended methods.

Well, how to do this? One way is to begin with conscious figures. Students already use "You're a rat, Charlie Brown." Their cars "scratch off." A school newspaper sports page includes the near-poetic "The Tiger backfield was a mud-spattered yet efficient machine." Students "choke up" on tests; they "pull" grades. A hamburger-joint hangout is "Endsville"; the "chick" they "wheel" there "soaks Cokes." The language they speak is filled with figure. The point is to make them conscious of it. You might then move toward deliberate use of figure. I once saw a teacher having students add seven lines to the one she'd written on the board: "The classroom is a prison, electronically controlled." That bold first line involved a lot of ordinarily diffident students. I saw a junior-high teacher work from commonplaces to complexities, beginning with the sun—which yielded "The sun is a red-splashed tiger"—and ending with poetry: "Poetry is climbing a mountain."

The simplest way to involve youngsters in something that's even closer to what they think of as poetry is to begin from "a listing poem." You've read many listing poems; their abundance will surprise you. You know Rupert Brooke's catalog in "The Great Lover." Fifteen-year-old Barbara Fainstein listed her own loved things.

These Have I Loved

These have I loved: warm rain dripping over tile roofs,
green frogs bellowing from lily pads;
pink peonies damp with cool dew drops;
wet grass between my toes;
crinkly paper;
red ink;
chubby, blond-haired children building sand castles;
mud puddles moving as the wind makes tiny ripples across
    them;
large footprints on wet sand,
the sweet potato cart on bitter city streets;
cold nights and warm, woolly blankets;
light wind upon my face;
wet paint brushes on rough rice paper;
old men on park benches feeding the flocking pigeons;
silence.

You know Elizabeth Browning's sonnet beginning, "How do I love thee?" You will see on page 52 Philip Booth's listing of railroad cars in "Crossing." Junior-high teachers know Elizabeth Coatsworth's "Swift Things Are Beautiful." The first verse reads:

Swift things are beautiful:
Swallows and deer,
And lightning that falls
Bright veined and clear,
Rivers and meteors,
Wind in the wheat,
The strong-withered horse,
The runner's sure feet.

Any student who can see this as a list of swift, beautiful things can make his own list of things. The list is first just a list. Then the listed items are made concrete and rich. Some items seem to lend themselves to figures of speech. These things I like; these things I don't. Very well. There are two stanzas paralleling Coatsworth's swift and slow things. Hard things and soft things? Tall things and short? Nasty things and nice? Any of these can produce facts, opinions, concrete details. An ordering principle suggests itself; items are shuffled; an almost-poem is accomplished. Lists can be polished and made richer for however long a time student interest perseveres.

Long lists resulting from the listing technique will often become short poems after you and the student writer's classmates help cull out the unnecessaries, the ungainlies, and the unworthies. From lists come near-poems, poems, and an appreciation for what it is the poet does. Try the listing game.

Other techniques for getting youngsters to say something poetically may better serve you. Have a student learn what a ballad is and try writing one about the deeds of a local hero. Have other students put the last line onto a limerick. Older students might try epigrams and couplets. With every teacher who helps students attempt to write something poetic, I cherish the delight and energy that goes into a haiku-writing session.

The study of good "professional" haiku would effectively reveal what it is and what it can achieve. Careful reading of such distinguished poets as Basho and Issa will help students achieve the moment of wonder and the genuine grace of haiku. Although some teachers unduly emphasize its form, the three-line stanza and syllable pattern of Japanese haiku (5–7–5) interests students: They enjoy solving the formal puzzle.

The haiku following, the work of Sally Andreson, a ninth-grader of Clarence, Iowa, nicely demonstrates successful student writing.

Fall

> The geese flying south
> In a row long and V-shaped
> Pulling in winter.

Sally Andreson tried (and in my judgment succeeded) to say something poetically. I suspect that because Sally has tried making a poem, she is a better, more sympathetic reader of poetry than students who have never squinted out an image or happened onto a metaphor of their own making.

Principle nine: Students must be helped to discover that poetry is written about many things. The subjects of poetry are not comprehended by nightingales, daffodils, anticipations of death, man's yen for life at sea, and the romantic love of landlubbers. Poetry is also about city streets, juke boxes, oil barges, and cars; hunting, prize fighting, rockets, and wars. Students need to learn well that the subjects of poetry come out of the very things that they see and know, that the language of poetry depends on contemporary and available sources for its nonliteralness, that the writers of poetry include well-groomed ladies and short-haired men who share the 1960's with them.

Perhaps I create this principle to make explicit what has been implied earlier; that is, making our students voluntary readers of poetry implies exposing them to considerable contemporary poetry. Perhaps half of the verse read and studied in junior-high grades should be of recent—post-World War II—vintage. Perhaps somewhat less recent verse can be justified for high-school juniors and seniors with college aspirations. We seem to forget that only occasionally do we teach students who will become tomorrow's literary scholars, poets, and English teachers; we regularly teach students whose lives can be made fuller and richer if we can persuade them that poetry has something for them. The chance for such persuasion will increase if we shorten the linguistic and cultural distances between today's student and poetry.

I argue, then, for poems that reveal today's excitements and situations, subjects and ideas both lovely and ugly. I urge teaching poems made up of today's metaphors and diction. Most teaching of poetry at any grade level might begin by confronting, in language however complex, what students care about, what is close to them in time and sound.

How do students learn that poetry is written about many things? By reading and getting involved with poems that represent the breadth of subject matters of recent and current poets. Where will the poems come from? From magazines fat and fancy, from others thin and temporal. From the occasional paperback collections of new poems that vie with Ian Fleming and Frank Yerby in drug stores, bus depots, and publishers' catalogs. (A subscription to Bowker's *Paperbound Books in Print* is a step-saving bargain for the searcher.) From whatever sources the teacher-reader-innovator—or his students—can find.

Josephine Miles, in *The English Journal*,[10] writes: "We need from modern poetry what we are not yet getting from it—a profession of the new meanings to be found in our new lives. When I

---

10. Volume LII, Number 4, April 1963, pp. 243–246.

mention the sorts of meanings I mean, you will laugh, because you will think them unpoetic. . . . And you will think them inhuman. . . . What can be seen and felt on a freeway, for example? What is the relevant timing in a jet flight? How do computing machines reflect thinking? How do we enthrall ourselves about the moon and Mars? What will leadership by television mean to our sense of politics? These are not the nonpoetry but the potential poetry of life, and we need them."

"The great virtue of the so-called angry and beat poets is," according to Professor Miles, "that they have had the energy to spell out the negatives, the nightmare." She calls for "a public poetry of the immediate future, following the private poetry of the immediate past."

Here's a poem that demonstrates my belief in searching out fresh poems. Poetry *is* about many things; this poem's about poetry. But it surprises us with its diction and metaphor.

The Loser

> and the next I remembered I'm on a table,
> everybody's gone: the head of bravery
> under light, scowling, flailing me down . . .
> and then some toad stood there, smoking a cigar:
> "Kid you're no fighter," he told me,
> and I got up and knocked him over a chair;
> it was like a scene in a movie, and
> he stayed there on his big rump and said
> over and over: "Jesus, Jesus, whatsamatta wit
> you?" and I got up and dressed,
> the tape still on my hands, and when I got home
> I tore the tape off my hands and
> wrote my first poem,
> and I've been fighting
> ever since.
>
> CHARLES BUKOWSKI

Bukowski's poem may prove a point even though there are communities and classrooms wherein "The Loser" might be just that.

Now for wiser counsel from poets Robert Francis and Philip Booth. Although both poets are, in general terms, arguing for pleasure with poetry and for close reading of poetry, it's possible to particularize what each is doing. Robert Francis sets up and then exercises an analogy between reading a poem and participating in a sport. The parallels he establishes suggest concrete ways that poems might be taught. Poetry and sports share, to a lesser or greater degree, discipline, strenuousness, competition, rules, and form; in both poetry and sports, excellence can be distinguished from incompetence.

Philip Booth urges us to go directly to poems (while sidestepping the teaching of things *about* poetry) and demonstrates his belief in the Socratic method through very sharp questions about poems of his own. His discussion of the fusing of image and idea will help many teachers read and teach poetry effectively.

Since I am responsible for selecting the poems discussed in the two essays following, I here make explicit my belief that all six poems are prime candidates for classroom teaching.

BIOGRAPHICAL NOTE

Robert Francis lives alone in his one-man house, Fort Juniper, on a wooded knoll four miles from Amherst Center, Massachusetts. He solves the economic problem of being an independent and unattached poet by doing all his own work and enjoying it.

With an A.B. from Harvard College and an Ed.M. from the Harvard Graduate School of Education, he thought he was going to spend his life in teaching. But his formal teaching has consisted of two years in secondary schools (one of them in Beirut, Lebanon) and a year and a half of college teaching. During the past decade he has taught poetry at summer writers' conferences.

The word *hobby* is not in his vocabulary. Yet he plays violin and piano and does small-scale gardening.

Asked about his honors, he says that his head has been bruised by very few falling plums. He was Phi Beta Kappa poet at Tufts in 1955 and at Harvard in 1960 and was awarded a Rome Fellowship from the American Academy of Arts and Letters for 1957–1958.

His books:

Stand With Me Here	Macmillan, 1936
Valhalla and Other Poems	Macmillan, 1938
The Sound I Listened For	Macmillan, 1944
We Fly Away	Swallow-Morrow, 1948
The Face Against the Glass	Private, 1950
The Orb Weaver	Wesleyan, 1960
Come Out Into the Sun	University of Massachusetts, 1965

He writes so often about athletes, he explains, because in the athlete's combination of youth, health, and peak effort he finds a perfect counterpoise to death.

This modest note was written by Robert Francis.

PART TWO

Poetry
as *Disciplined*
Play
Robert Francis

Someday in your class, perhaps when things aren't going too well,
suggest that reading a poem well is like participating in some sport
requiring real skill. Consider how fine a day it would be if every-
body in your class knew as much about poetry as he does, say, about
baseball. Few students have to be told what baseball is or what it is
good for. Posing parallels between poetry and sports might help
get the class into motion without its usual misconceptions and in-
hibitions.

Are there real similarities between sports and poetry? Both are
kinds of play as distinct from work. Agreed. But they are play *disciplined* and often *strenuous*, sometimes far more strenuous than
almost any work. Bright Thirteen asks: "Is poetry strenuous—just
to read it?" The answer might be another question: "Is chess strenuous?" There is more than one kind of strenuousness. To be excited
by poetry, a student must first encounter exciting poems; but he
also has to know how to follow a poem play by play—hits, strategies,
and all the rest.

Extra-bright Fifteen observes: "Sports are more exciting than
poetry because any game you are watching is always a new game and
is taking place right before your eyes; any poem you are reading is
finished, deadened by print, probably years old." Counter with the
idea that one of the exciting things about an exciting poem (or any
other work of art) is precisely that it *can* be read (or looked at or

The first half of Mr. Francis' essay, in slightly different form, appeared in *The English Journal*
(November 1963) as "Poetry as [Disciplined] Play" by Stephen Dunning and Robert Francis.

listened to) over and over and still be exciting. One test of art is its inexhaustibility.

Slugging Outfielder pins you to the wall with another difference. "Sports have competition. There's usually a winner and a loser. With poetry," and this with narrowed eyes, "the only losers are the kids who have to read it." (Slugger deserves the chuckle he gets!) Surely competition and exercise are the chief points of sports. And though there is competition in the arts, it is only incidental. We won't tell Slugger, "Life is a game, boy, that must be played according to the rules." But we might say that fine performance in an athlete *is* praised in and for itself. In some sports, competition is secondary; a golfer often competes with par and with his own past performances; gymnasts compete against a point system and only secondarily against each other. Isn't this like the competition among poets?

Competing not so much with one another
As with perfection.

If this doesn't kill discussion altogether, you might seek this agreement: Sports surpass the arts in some respects; the arts surpass sports in others. Poetry and baseball are alike and are different. In both sports and art the fundamental motive for playing and watching is enjoyment, exhilaration.

"OK. If the purpose of poetry is enjoyment," tries Stolid Sixteen, "why not make it an extracurricular activity?" You fix Stolid Sixteen with your "Don't get smart-alecky" stare. "I try to make some classroom activities enjoyable," you say, making it clear through intonation that you don't favor sustained revelries. But Sixteen's question is a good one. You can use it. Students know the place to learn rules is in the classroom. If you suggest that there are rules in poetry to be learned and obeyed just as there are rules in games and sports, many students will accept your statement unquestioningly. But the measure of truth in this statement conceals a larger measure of untruth.

Rules in poetry there certainly are. If you set out to write a sonnet, the rules prescribe fourteen lines of iambic pentameter, a choice among certain rhyme schemes, and so forth. These are indeed rules, but what we need to keep in mind is that they are rules that nobody is compelled or obliged to obey. To write a sonnet in strict form, you follow the rules. But if you want to change or modify the rules, who is to say you nay? The healthy growth of poetry from age to age requires constant experimentation and a willingness to be new even when the new may seem very strange. Not all great poets, but many of them, have been notable breakers of rules.

It is neither a crime nor a sin to write a poem of thirteen or fifteen lines and call it a sonnet. There might be a legitimate argument, of course, as to whether it might not be better called something else.

If a poet does not write any sonnets at all, he is still faced with choices. He may if he wishes choose some other type or pattern with its own rules. Or he may make up rules of his own, as would be the case if he originated a new stanza form. Or he may write without being conscious of any rules. But if what he writes is a true poem, it will be controlled and disciplined in some way. (By this time, Stolid Sixteen has forgotten what question he asked and is deep in private thought.)

Then Valedictorian and Salutatorian in chorus: "Can you say a poem is controlled and disciplined if it does not follow given rules?"

A poet is someone who has an urge not only to express something but also to fashion and mold it. He wants to make what he is saying as shapely as an artistic vase, as effective as a fine tool, as sharp as an arrow. He would like all parts of his poem — words, lines, stanzas, thoughts, metaphors, rhythms — working in perfect harmony and cooperation. The interconnections and cooperations of all parts of a poem may be called its *form*, because the poem was *formed* by the working out of all these relationships. Organization is another possible word, though this word scarcely suggests the intricacy and delicacy of the process and the result.

How does form in poetry compare with form in sports? Many a young athlete could tell you better than you can tell him. But is it far off the track to suggest that a diver's or a pitcher's or a skier's form is a certain way of holding and moving the body which has proved by experience to be most efficient? A kind of stylized and rhythmic movement in which there is no waste effort and no interference of one part by another? The athlete organizes his body, the poet organizes his poem.

Although the next-period buzzer has sounded, everyone but the hall monitor, diligently about his duties, has his own example of athlete (or artist) whose unique form contributed to success: the tennis star with the two-handed backhand, the basketballer with the over-the-head free throw, the batter with his foot in the bucket, Whoozis with his poems that have no capital letters, Shakespeare! But no one of these stars breaks *all* the rules of form. The batter keeps his eye on the ball; Whoozis knows form so intimately that he can play with it. You drive home the point: Structure and pattern and organization exist to be modified.

Some argue that only the poet should be concerned with how his poem is put together and that the reader should be concerned only with what it says. This is a mistaken view. Pleasure in reading a poem comes partly from being sensitive to a poem's pattern of sound, its nice balances and contrasts, from catching those happy instances where a poem is doing what it is saying.

The beauty of this kind of appreciation is that it is not a matter of guessing and speculation. The pattern is right there in black and white on the page. For this reason, pattern and structure and form (in their simpler aspects) are good things to emphasize while studying poems. These concrete details help focus on the poem itself and prevent wandering too far afield.

Perhaps there has already been too much talk about poetry without reference to a poem. In another class period you might put the following poem on the board and discuss some aspects of its structure. (I hope it isn't loading the dice to continue the poetry-as-play idea through discussion of a poem that is apparently a baseball poem.) Here is "Pitcher."

Pitcher

His art is eccentricity, his aim	1
How not to hit the mark he seems to aim at,	2
His passion how to avoid the obvious,	3
His technique how to vary the avoidance.	4
The others throw to be comprehended. He	5
Throws to be a moment misunderstood.	6
Yet not too much. Not errant, arrant, wild,	7
But every seeming aberration willed.	8
Not to, yet still, still to communicate	9
Making the batter understand too late.	10

First make sense of some of the harder words, especially those in lines 7 and 8. The classroom athletes can then be prominently involved in primitive paraphrase. The first couplet suggests curve balls and spitters, the fast ball and the control that allows the pitcher to mix up his throws and avoid the batter's bat. The second couplet pins this down. It is the pitcher's *passion* to throw a slow pitch when the batter expects a fast one, his *technique* to have a variety of pitches ready for controlled use. Line 5 says that everyone but the pitcher throws to be caught. The third baseman, taking a hot grounder, whips the ball to the "comprehending" first baseman. But in line 6, clearly, the pitcher's unique function is explained: if he isn't a "moment misunderstood" by batters, he'll be knocked out of the ball game.

Lines 7 and 8 speak of the smallness of the difference between pitches; they talk again about control. ("How big is the strike zone, Freddie?" "What is a *seeming* aberration?") And in lines 9 and 10 the batter has swung and missed; only after the ball is safely in the catcher's mitt does the batter understand the pitch.

"That's paraphrase enough," you might say. "Look at the rhyme scheme. A poem as short as this might be expected to be rhyming couplets. Rhyme would help give a tight weave to the poem, a sense of finish. But there are other devices for weaving a poem together. It would be a pity if you failed to see what was here simply because something else wasn't."

The strategy in this poem is to end with a rhyme and to build up to it. "Pitcher" clearly rhymes its final couplet: *communicate* and *late* make a strict, full rhyme. *Wild* and *willed* do not rhyme, yet are obviously close in sound. *Comprehend* and *misunderstood* have no chiming sound but provide a sharp antonymous contrast. Students will see these three points clearly enough. In the second couplet "avoid the obvious" and "vary the avoidance" balance each other because of *avoid* and *avoidance* and the play on the letter *v*. In the first couplet there is the repetition of *aim* in *aim at.*

"But," protests the student, "you have me reading the poem backward—parts of it, at least. The end sounds."

One reason that poetry belongs in the classroom is that it can be framed. "Pitcher," for example, has ten lines. They can be read from top to bottom, from bottom to top. Students can see the whole poem at once, can keep it all in mind. They can look at every word, at word play and at rhyme, at subject matter and at metaphor. Perhaps we shouldn't be stuffy about reading poems backward; poets sometimes write them backward.

To return to poetry as play (and perhaps stretch the comparison too far), beginning a poem without rhyme and building up to it creates an effect like building up to a climax in a sports event. The final rhyme of "Pitcher" comes like the smack of the ball in the catcher's mitt—if not the crack of the ball against the bat. Ask students, "What is rhyme exactly? When is rhyme rhyme and when is it something else? And can 'something else' serve a poem as usefully and as effectively as strict rhyme?" Ask whether the chime between *communicate* and *late* is any more effective—or more sacred—than the chime between *wild* and *willed.* We have already decided that rules of form are made to be broken. So with rules of rhyme.

Students know that poets have an intense interest in words.

They may not know that that interest extends to the sound and shape of words as well as to their meaning. The accidental peculiarities of words, little oddities that we generally ignore or joke about, are put to use in poetry. (Thus *errant* and *arrant* in line 7.) Rhyme is only one of many linguistic oddities.

It's important that students have the experience of talking about such things as form and rhyme. *Very* young people tend to equate rhyme with poetry. Junior-high youngsters are likely to appreciate poems that rhyme and yet grant that some nonrhyming poems are all right. Most inexperienced readers of poetry, even in college, are likely to look askance at anything in between rhyme and nonrhyme. What is sometimes called "slant rhyme" or "half rhyme" is to inexperienced readers "sour rhyme." They know *trolley* and *bully* aren't perfect chimes. Has the poet a tin ear? Students need experience with "slant rhyme." Inexperienced readers need to be induced away from limited tastes. Such readers need to read, argue, and debate rhymes; textbook definitions of versification are a (perhaps unnecessary) second step.

If your discussion of rhyme has already dissipated any pleasure students felt on first seeing "Pitcher," the poem should now be erased from the chalkboard. Time instead for some work with verbals or with sentence variety. But if any ergs of poetry energy remain, a more complicated question should be asked: "Is this a baseball poem and nothing else?"

Suggest, for discussion, that "Pitcher" is really a poem about poetry. Or, better, suggest that the reader might take it equally as a poem about poetry and baseball. The poem shows the pitcher putting his curves on the ball; it also shows the poet putting *his* curves on language. The poem might allow you to argue—back to sports and poetry—that the two things are in some respects so close together that a poem about one of them can also be a poem about the other.

"How might the poem be about poetry, too?" If there is a response, persist: "Is this poem equally true about both pitcher and poet?" Students will be interested in knowing whether the poet intended this "double-header" possibility. (He did.) They may wonder whether what seem like peculiarities of language are deliberate or happen in spite of the poet. In short, "Is the poet-pitcher wild, or has he control?" "What about *errant* and *arrant*?" "Are these good pitches or bad?"

The principle of involving students in considering a poem rather than learning "right answers" through explication is important. One student who got pretty deeply involved in the poem felt that it broke down at the end. The student felt that the poet was trying to fool the reader.

If that's the effect of the poem, it may mean the poem is a bad one. It might be argued, though, that the poet is trying to keep the reader surprised, not trying to fool him. Surprise always comes too late to be anticipated. How else could it be surprise? But it does not come too late for enjoyment, for the enjoyment depends largely on the surprise.

Poetry and play? The man in the bleachers is, by empathy or sympathy, pitching with the pitcher, batting with the batter, and running with the runner; the reader of poetry, if he is fairly alive and awake, is writing the poem with the poet.

If it was something of a surprise for your class to discover that poetry has much in common with sports, it may surprise them again to hear that poems can be like detective stories. I'm thinking not so much of "difficult" poems, that have to be put under the microscope to be read at all, as of poems that look easy but raise questions that cannot be answered except by a little detective work, like this one:

Summons

> Keep me from going to sleep too soon
> Or if I go to sleep too soon
> Come wake me up. Come any hour
> Of night. Come whistling up the road.
> Stomp on the porch. Bang on the door.
> Make me get out of bed and come
> And let you in and light a light.
> Tell me the northern lights are on
> And make me look. Or tell me clouds
> Are doing something to the moon
> They never did before, and show me.
> See that I see. Talk to me till
> I'm half as wide awake as you
> And start to dress wondering why
> I ever went to bed at all.
> Tell me the walking is superb.
> Not only tell me but persuade me.
> You know I'm not too hard persuaded.

Most of us don't enjoy being waked out of a sound sleep. After we've gone to bed for the night, we don't want anybody banging on the door. Yet here is someone who asks for it, begs for it. How come? What is his motive? And where in the poem do you find the clue to it? A detective, remember, can make use of very small clues, but he has to have something definite nevertheless. Mere guessing won't get him anywhere.

If I were teaching your class, I'd begin with this question: Why does X want Y to wake him up or keep him awake? I'd welcome as many answers as possible. I might write them on the board. Here is one way the discussion might work out:

PUPIL A. X doesn't want to miss the northern lights or any unusual cloud-and-moon display. That's his reason. It says so right in the poem.

PUPIL B. Then why wouldn't X go back to bed after seeing the sights? Why would he want to go walking with Y?

PUPIL C. It's neither the northern lights nor the walk, but a chance to visit with his good friend Y. It's friendship.

PUPIL D. If it's a visit with Y that he wants most of all, why wait till after midnight? Why not daytime?

PUPIL E *(bursting with conviction).* Listen, this guy wants to be waked up for the sake of being waked up. *(Laughter)* And what's so funny about that? He wants to live, and you're only half alive (if even that much) when you're asleep. It's life he wants, and so naturally he wants somebody to help keep him from wasting his life in snoozing. Look how the poem starts. Come talk with me? No! Come walk with me? No! Come see the northern lights? No! The poem starts:

Keep me from going to sleep too soon
Or if I go to sleep too soon
Come wake me up!

PUPIL F *(almost persuaded but not wanting to agree too easily).* But when is too soon? When is it too soon to go to sleep?

PUPIL E. Any time is too soon to go to sleep if there's something worth staying awake for. Any time's too soon if you've got a friend who can make you forget you're sleepy. You might as well ask when it's too soon to die.

TEACHER. Wait a moment. You're getting very warm but I don't know that you've got the answer in the bag yet. X does want to be waked up for the sake of being waked up, just as you say. But he wants Y to do the waking. Otherwise an alarm clock would do just as well. Or anybody else banging on the door after midnight. Pupil

C was right: It is a visit with Y that X wants. But Pupil A was right too: X wants Y to show him or tell him something exciting. It's all these things together, isn't it? Isn't that what the poem adds up to — without saying it in so many words?

The trouble, of course, with my butting in this way is the danger you'll think I must be right since I wrote the poem. But I'm trying not to take any unfair advantage. I want to be just a good reader of a poem I happen to have written myself. I mean to be a good detective getting all my clues from the poem itself (and from what general knowledge I have of human nature).

Just as the detective "reconstructs the crime," so we reconstruct the poem, or rather, the situation in the poem. Here goes. Y is young. Right? One bit of evidence is that he comes "whistling up the road." Young, alert, and enthusiastic. X is older, perhaps much older. Evidence? The way he talks. No kid talks like that. Whatever else X finds agreeable in his young friend, he especially values his being young, alert, enthusiastic. X hopes to catch a little enthusiasm from Y? Is glad to be waked out of sleep by Y because Y has already waked him up a little when he was *not* sleeping?

Have you noticed (have you detected) how this poem consists of one command after another? What does this repetition do? Give force to the poem, like a boxer's punches? Not only repetition of commands but repetition of certain words of command: *come, come, come, tell me, tell me.* What do you say to this?

But somebody else has something to say, I think, a girl who hasn't said anything yet but who has taken everything in.

GIRL (*very quietly now*). All the things that X asks Y to do sound as if Y had already done them. How would X know just what to ask Y to do if Y hadn't done some of them at least once before? What I mean is, Y has already come whistling up the road some night not long before, banged on the door, and waked X out of his sleep to tell him about the northern lights and the clouds. X is simply asking for a repeat. Not asking him face to face, probably, but asking him in thought.

Such a girl (or boy), if you had one in your class, would make me want to keep still and listen.

Here's another poem that wants a little detective work done on it.

Sing a Song of Juniper

Sing a song of juniper
Whose song is seldom sung,
Whose needles prick the finger,
Whose berries burn the tongue.

Sing a song of juniper
With boughs shaped like a bowl
For holding sun or snowfall
High on the pasture knoll.

Sing a song of juniper
Whose green is more than green,
Is blue and bronze and violet
And colors in between.

Sing a song of juniper
That keeps close to the ground,
A song composed of silence
And very little sound.

Sing a song of juniper
That hides the hunted mouse,
And gives me outdoor shadows
To haunt my indoor house.

Are we supposed to like this juniper? Does the speaker in the
poem like it himself? If he does like it and wants us to like it, why
talk about needles that prick the finger and berries that burn the
tongue? Who wants his fingers pricked and his tongue burnt?
Couldn't he paint a more flattering picture?

Somebody (I think a girl) says, "Maybe you like juniper and
maybe you don't, but I'm sure the man in the poem likes it."
BOY. How do you know? Where's your evidence?
GIRL. Well, he certainly doesn't sound as if he hated it. And if
he felt only so-so, would he bother to write a poem about it?
BOY. So he likes it because he doesn't hate it?
GIRL. He makes juniper interesting.
BOY. For instance?
GIRL. Interesting shape like a bowl. Interesting colors. Strong
character — keeps close to the ground.

BOY. And pricks the finger?

3RD PARTY. He likes it in spite of the fact that it pricks the finger.

GIRL. But look, you don't have to let it prick your finger, do you? You can be careful, can't you?

BOY. And burns the tongue?

TEACHER (*who hasn't been able to get in a word before*). Ever taste a ripe juniper berry? No? Looks like a blueberry and tastes like anything but.

GIRL. But you don't have to taste it unless you want to, do you?

TEACHER. Fact is, I like the taste. Very hot and spicy. I like to chew a berry, but I don't swallow it.

3RD PARTY. Candied ginger burns the tongue a little, too, but it's delicious.

BOY. So all this is supposed to make me like juniper? But that hiding the hunted mouse, *that* doesn't make me love it particularly.

GIRL. That's because you're not a mouse.

BOY. Thanks!

Such a free-for-all can open up a poem as well as loosen tongues. I think it's often a good way to begin but not so often a good way to end—unless you want to end out beyond left field in the tall grass hunting for a lost ball.

TEACHER (*finally taking his innings*). He *likes juniper in spite of the fact it pricks the finger.* One of you said that a minute ago. Reminds me of a good friend of mine. He can be very sharp at times, even cutting. But I accept it as part of his personality. I don't say I like him *in spite of it*—I really wouldn't want him any different. Perhaps the man in the poem feels that way about juniper. Like a friend. Somebody he's lived near long enough to know and understand. He takes the personality whole. Wouldn't really want it any different. Does that make sense?

There's no certainty, of course, that you as teacher—or I as poet—or anyone else is right as to a poem's meaning. I hope you're glad this is so, glad that you can't turn to the back of the book for *the* answer. When it comes to insight and mother-wit, a teacher is no more privileged than any student in his class. For this reason teaching poetry can spur a sense of sportsmanship in teacher and pupil alike, a respect for any honest opinion, however wild or childish-seeming.

But have we done all this talking without coming face to face with juniper itself? Juniper, that tough, wild, low-growing, swirl-shaped evergreen that farmers hate for the way it takes over an entire pasture and leaves less and less room for the edible grass? Who knows juniper? Who can say if this poem describes it accurately? Who will bring to class a branch of it for observation (and risk a pricked finger)?

Another thing. Over and over the poem keeps saying, "Sing a song of juniper." But what else is the poem itself but a song of juniper? It wouldn't be hard to make up a little tune and sing it. What makes this poem more singable, more *lyric*, than some poems? Its rhythm, which you could almost call singsong? Its rhymes? Anything else?

Finally, to get back to an early question: Couldn't the poet paint a more flattering picture of juniper if he wants us to like it? Perhaps flattering is just what this poet doesn't want to be. Truth seems to be good enough for him. Since he likes juniper, he naturally likes the truth about it. But even if he didn't happen to like juniper, I suspect he'd still like the truth.

To be truthful but not obvious — that seems to be the trick. To be as full of surprises as the baseball pitcher, but to surprise us with the truth. To make us see what we never saw before. Perhaps to make us like (or at least appreciate) what we never thought we could like. Do all poets have this power to surprise us, not only with exciting words but with new attitudes? Or only some poets?

Philip Booth, born in 1925, grew up in the New Hampshire foothills and on the Maine coast. Graduated from Dartmouth after Air Force service in World War II, he holds an M.A. from Columbia and is now an Associate Professor of English at Syracuse University.

His nonteaching interests include writing poetry, skiing (he was a varsity skier at Dartmouth), and sailing. Such honors as a Guggenheim Memorial Fellowship, election as Phi Beta Kappa poet at Columbia University, and the *Saturday Review* poetry prize have come to him. His first book of poetry, *Letter from a Distant Land*, won the Lamont Prize of the Academy of American Poets. His second book of poetry, *The Islanders*, was nominated for the National Book Award.

His books:

Letter from a Distant Land	Viking, 1957
The Islanders	Viking, 1961
Weathers and Edges	Viking, 1966

His poems have appeared in most major literary journals in America and England. A second Guggenheim, in 1965, made it possible for him to complete his third collection.

PART THREE

Image
and
Idea

Philip Booth

My poem "Crossing" begins "STOP   LOOK   LISTEN." These three words are what any good poem makes implicit. The best poems, like the best teachers, don't need attention-demanding words; they command pause by the intensity of their language, they make demanding images for the mind's eye and speak in a rhythm wholly their own. But just as "Crossing" begins by making explicit what a great poem can leave unsaid, so teachers less wise than Socrates must sometimes demand, explicitly, the kind of attention which young students are still half unwilling to give. Students new to poetry need the support of a teacher's most imaginative questioning if they are to stop, look, and listen as they read.

As a poet who has stopped, looked, and listened in writing his poems, I'd like to support Socratic teaching by suggesting the kinds of questions that might usefully be asked of those poems. Having taught "Crossing" in public schools, I know that few principals (and fewer school boards) know what goes on in a good teacher's good class. Every man must teach in the ways he has found most naturally useful, and I least of all want to play principal in suggesting how three of my own poems might be approached. Infinite variations might profitably be played on the specific questions I'll raise; but the attitude represented by such questions has worked for me, and I want to argue its value as a way of stretching students to read poems beyond my own.

Crossing

STOP LOOK LISTEN
as gate stripes swing down,
count the cars hauling distance
upgrade through town:
warning whistle, bellclang,
engine eating steam,
engineer waving,
a fast-freight dream:
B&M boxcar,
boxcar again,
Frisco gondola,
eight-nine-ten,
Erie and Wabash,
Seabord, U.P.
Pennsy tankcar,
twenty-two, three,
Phoebe Snow, B&O,
thirty-four, five,
Santa Fe cattle,
shipped alive,
red cars, yellow cars,
orange cars, black,
Youngstown steel
down to Mobile
on Rock Island track,
fifty-nine, sixty,
hoppers of coke,
Anaconda copper,
hotbox smoke,
eighty-eight,
red-ball freight,
Rio Grande,
Nickel Plate,
Hiawatha,
Lackawanna,
rolling fast
and loose,
ninety-seven,,
coal car,
boxcar,
CABOOSE!

Starting students on "Crossing," I'd not permit myself any advance talk about poetry as a special "art," I'd give no advance assignment of this particular poem, and I'd begin where the poem begins, with its title and first line. Let the least teacher, even, read aloud the first three words of "Crossing," and even his least student will more or less imagine the possibility of a train. Ask such a student what he'd put in a poem about a train (which began "STOP LOOK LISTEN"), and the girl next to him will say "Box-cars!" Ask Red in the back row if he'd begin this poem about a train with boxcars, and he'll fill in what must surely begin both the train and the poem. Ask what else beyond an engine and boxcars might be involved in a train poem which began "STOP LOOK LISTEN" and—because students can be asked to imagine more rather than less—they'll have half written "Crossing" before a teacher finds time to read it aloud. The demand on students to *stop*, and to *look*, will work for any teacher who plays his class as a poet plays his lines, by ear.

The best teacher's best good luck would be, in this particular case, to have his listeners tell him—before he read "Crossing"—that "a train poem ought to sound like a train." But even after reading, a good teacher lacking good luck would ask his students what the poem included that they forgot. Particularly if they're seventh-graders, they probably forgot to *listen*. Yet even if they missed the sound which the rhythm of the poem comes to, they'll need only an imaginative question to show them that the pace of the rhythm is (with the breaks for counting) a determining factor in the poem's form. Let talk about meter or onomatopoeia, if somebody's syllabus demands it, be incidental at most. If students aren't burdened with too much Greek, they may even be satisfied that the form the poem sets itself comes whole: that this train poem which begins "STOP LOOK LISTEN" fulfills not only its form but also the subject announced by its title.

"Crossing" is the simplest of poems (simple enough, even, once to have been used as an advertisement that might stop tired commuters flipping full pages of *Time*), and too much talk would both sidetrack and wreck it. But I use it as an example of what I most want to make explicit: that image and idea are finally inseparable in a first-rate poem. If "Crossing" is first-rate at all, it is of course only so in the very low order of patter-poems. But even "Crossing" involves that organic interrelationship of feeling and thought which I call "image and idea," and some sense of how "Crossing" began may, I hope, start good teachers toward teaching any poem well.

Although part of the "idea" of this poem happened to occur to me before I sensed the primary image which charged me to write it, I discovered (or rediscovered) the meaning of that idea only in the actual process of writing. An image, then, began the poem for me *as a poem*, and I am sure that "image" precedes "idea" for most poets as they write their best poems. This does not mean, of course, that "idea" necessarily follows "image" in poems as they are finally printed; the fusion of image and idea is more complex than a simple matter of sequence. But just as a poet explores his images to discover—*in the process of writing*—what idea evolves from them, so I am convinced that the process of reading must *begin* with an examination of images and *continue* with how the images interrelate.

"Crossing" began for me (although it had not yet begun as a poem) in a small newsstand next to an upcountry railroad track, where the train which delivered newspapers was always made up of freight as well as mail cars. I used to see the names of far places on the sides of boxcars as the train slowed on a slight incline and the crossing gates swung down in front of that newsstand. Whether I then thought of beginning a poem about those boxcars, I can't now be sure. But I kept the images of place names, engine, and gate stripes in my mind's eye, and I can remember thinking something close to what was a first "idea" of the poem: I recognized that, for me, the newsstand freight seemed to be "hauling distance upgrade" into my own experience.

I might now argue, in retrospect, that the function of "Crossing" is to haul the distances of childhood experience upgrade into a reader's memory. My present concern is, however, to demonstrate that there would have been no poem without some *other* imagistic impression with which my first images and my tentative "idea" might combine. Had I known, then, that the poem awaited a major image, I wouldn't have known where to look for it. I think I simply bought my newspaper and went home, no more a poet than anybody who stores in his mind some unexamined images.

Three years later, when I was riding the Silver Meteor north through the yards on the New York side of Trenton, a freight on a parallel track slid slowly past my Pullman. Under me, I could hear the Meteor's wheels bump over the fishplates, but my ear's further recognition was in the names on the two boxcars beside my grimy window. *Hiawatha* went by me, followed by *Lackawanna*: a magic and an industrial name, literally coupled; together, they repeated the exact rhythm of the wheels on the fishplates under my feet. If an image can, as I take it, appeal to any of man's five and country senses (not only to his eye), then I think I can claim that the way those train names imposed their rhythm on my ear was to become the central image of "Crossing" and to dictate its ultimate form. But only in that coincident instant when I remembered my newsstand crossing did the poem begin to take shape in my mind. "Lackawanna" meant distance to me as well as rhythm; "Hiawatha" owned comparable rhythm and also presented itself as a name thick with the magic of childhood. All these images and minimal "ideas" began to seem interrelated; as I tried to order their relationships by writing, my memory of the newsstand crossing resolved itself to begin to be the poem called "Crossing."

No reader should need to know the genesis of a poem in order to read it well; my present use of "Crossing" is merely to suggest how—in even the most minor poem—a poet begins to write by exploring images for whatever idea reveals itself in their interrelationships. As an image is *felt*, and an idea intellectually *known*, it's possible to talk about this process in terms of "bringing the mind to bear on what the heart feels." Bringing the mind to bear involves, of course, those techniques of ordering and structuring which shape a poem into an organic whole.

But young readers should not, I think, be burdened with concerns of structure or technique. Young readers will be most wholly rewarded by a teacher who asks of a poem's images the students' full response and who then, *only then*, asks further questions of what "idea" such interrelated images finally reveal. The question to pose to students starting poetry is not (God forbid!) "What, in twenty-five words or less, is this poem's theme?" If there is a single question basic to all other questions concerning poetry, it might be this: "What are the images and ideas in this poem, and *how do they interrelate?*" This, as he writes, is the poet's problem; and the reader, reading a poem new to him, is faced with precisely the problem realized by a poet assimilating a new experience. Only as the poet recognizes, relates, and fuses the components of any experience does his poem begin to exist. Like his ultimate reader, he must stop, look, and listen with every possible faculty; the act of writing is for him an act of exploration and—he hopes—discovery. Like a four-year-old struggling with the inadequacies of his language to express what has newly impressed him, he uses words to explore what he thinks he feels.

If, as is rarely the case, the potential poem begins for him with an abstract idea, the poet unconsciously asks himself: How do I feel about what I partially know? More commonly, with a felt image in mind, he unconsciously asks: *What can I know about what I feel?* Selecting and reselecting images from the whole range of his experience, the poet writes and rewrites, reaching to discover what he can partially *know* in the chaos of his own feelings. But beyond his own needs for self-revelation, he wants to share what he feels he knows: he wants to charge his language with an emotional intensity comparable to the force of the experience which, as he has written it out, he knows he has come to recognize.

What can I know about what I feel? This is not merely a "poet's" question; it is (however unconsciously) the prime question that all human beings ask in their becoming human. By questioning charged images in whatever poem, a teacher not only can confirm his students' feelings but can (with luck) extend their sense of what they feel they know.

Poems either confirm or extend the feeling and knowing of their readers; some poems (like cummings') confirm knowing and extend feeling; great poems (say those of Yeats) extend a reader's knowing by first confirming what he partially feels. The images of "Crossing" perhaps confirm a reader's feeling about trains, but its "idea" extends his knowing little, if at all. "Maine," the second of three mechanically oriented poems I'll discuss here, seems to me to work by both confirmation and extension; "Propeller" (p. 60), although its first stanza asks confirmation by way of simple description, is most of all committed to extending its reader's response. The three poems are, in sequence, increasingly complex; but each involves its own fusion of image and idea, charged by my own exploration to induce in readers a discovery comparable to mine. It took me some sixty-seven draft pages to satisfy myself that "Propeller" had come whole and that I understood how I felt about the literal propeller which, in the process of the poem, becomes my metaphor for all beautiful objects that man can create. I can only hope that no reader needs sixty-seven readings to respond meaningfully to the poem.

But I doubt that any reader's response will be full on only a single reading, or even on two or three. Naïve readers repeatedly imagine that poems spring perfectly into being, as if from the brow of Zeus. Such readers pay perhaps unconscious tribute to the illusion of spontaneity for which the lyric poet strives, but they rarely extend themselves by asking of a good poem the questions that all good poems (like all complex experiences) deserve. To teach students how to ask such questions, even when those questions are not perfectly answerable, seems to me to be the role of any good teacher.

Ideally, of course, all questions a poem raises about itself should be answerable by the poem. If the parts of a poem come whole, those parts should be open to useful questioning—if such questioning not merely demands a rote analysis of, say, a stanza's rhyme scheme but is a means of discovering how image and idea are organically interrelated. Most of all, I suspect, a teacher moving readers toward poems should raise questions about each poem's language. Since the poet's attitude toward his experience should, in the reading of any poem, become part of the reader's response, the poet's *tone* is of primary importance; and only through the closest questioning of the poet's language can that tone be identified.

Maine

When old cars get retired, they go to Maine.
Thick as cows in backlots off the blacktop,
East of Bucksport, down the washboard
From Penobscot to Castine,
they graze behind frame barns: a Ford   5
turned tractor, Hudsons chopped to half-ton
trucks, and Chevy panels, jacked up,
tireless, geared to saw a cord of wood.

Old engines never die. Not in Maine,
where men grind valves the way their wives grind axes.   10
Ring-jobs burned-out down the Turnpike
still make revolutions, turned marine.
If Hardscrabble Hill makes her knock,
Maine rigs the water-jacket salt: a man
can fish forever on converted sixes,   15
and for his mooring, sink a V-8 block.

When fishing's poor, a man traps what he can.
Even when a one-horse hearse from Bangor fades
away, the body still survives:
painted lobster, baited—off Route 1—   20
with home preserves and Indian knives,
she'll net a parlor-full of Fords and haul in
transient Cadillacs like crabs. Maine trades
in staying power, not shiftless drives.

Looking at line 1 of "Maine" after a third or fourth reading, for instance, a class could surely be questioned as to the meaning (in context) of the single word *retired*. That a Maine image of retreaded tires on cars put out to pasture happened, in fact, to be the sudden fusion of image and idea which began my poem is far less important than that students realize how the poet's tone derives from his "meaning" not *either* retreading or retirement but *both*. How, comparably, does *tireless* function in line 8? Isn't its function both to confirm the meanings of *retired* and at the same time to extend such meanings toward the sense of preservation and survival made comic in the last stanza?

That the germ of the poem's theme is contained within the image of cars without tires was, for me, discovery and luck. A good teacher can make that luck a discovery for students, not so that they will want to memorize "Maine," but so that they may become capable of reading further poems with their own questions in mind. Mac the Knife in a back-corner classroom seat may, at most, be relieved to read about down-East mechanics rather than Shelley's sunsets. He may not catch my buried echo of the old song about old soldiers not dying but just fading away; but even he can be asked how the thick consonants of line 2 contribute to the total rhythmic effect of the first stanza. And Sally who's headed for Radcliffe, impatient as she may be with Maine lobstermen, can profitably be stopped by some question as to where and how the poet defines his own attitude toward Maine—which is, after all, the poem's announced subject.

The title of "Crossing" defines what the poem's images will be, and even a first reading will confirm this. "Maine" is more complex in that its images extend rather than confirm one's original sense of its title; the poem, in effect, talks about a geographical state (and a state of mind) in terms of old cars, even as it improbably uses *tireless* wheels (line 8) as an image of survival. Some of the verbal play within "Maine" is, of course, as simple as this sort of punning. But punning is fundamentally complex, in that it treats two concepts simultaneously *in terms of each other*, and it may be a profitable introduction to metaphor, that "talking about one thing in terms of another" which Robert Frost has called poetry's chief mode.

Metaphor, in this large sense, raises questions which few students know how to ask, and which teachers must repeatedly ask of them. High-schoolers who can recite dictionary definitions of simile and metaphor (and even synecdoche) are as innocent as Huck Finn about the *function* of metaphor. They, like Huck, use metaphor wildly and wonderfully in their most natural talk. They're poets in spite of themselves when they are most naturally articulate. But assign them a theme and they fall back on the dead metaphor of most clichés; question them about a poem's ambivalent image and they (who know by heart the table of valences) defend against extending themselves by insisting that whatever is ambivalent is meaninglessly ambiguous and/or impossibly untrue.

A teacher's role here must be, I submit, to play with language as poets play with it: to remind students by example that their own argot is highly metaphorical, and to demonstrate that a poet's skill can control metaphor to mean two things and only two. To ask of a poem's metaphors every possible question does not mean that every possible answer is "right"; the poet controls the multiplicity of meanings by context, and context must be a prime part of whatever question. How, for instance, does my play with wives who *grind axes* (line 10) recover itself from cliché and become a metaphor (as I trust it does) in the context of grinding *valves?* The question admits of no simple answer, since it (being compounded from two parts of a whole) is literally complex. But it is only by way of such questions, all of which should fundamentally ask how parts function in contributing toward a whole, that students can begin to see that a poem's complexity is no more nor less than one man's meaningfully ordered sense of the complex world which they, too, are learning to inhabit.

Poetry, as a merely literary phenomenon, interests me not at all, and students who are taught poetry as if it were separate from the world's reality (rather than part of it, even its essence) have my full sympathy. Poetry is as fundamental to the world, and to mankind, as chemistry — no matter how slightly the world and its inhabitants may choose to acknowledge either. That the most apparently disparate images and ideas admit of fusion is, to poets, as basic a knowledge as compounding from the Table of Elements is to chemists. That poets can control such fusion, so that image and idea compound to become organically new, is their claim to a literally vital human function. No poet can rightfully claim that his sense of reality supersedes the exterior reality of those trains, junked cars, and propellers (or whatever) which he celebrates. His celebration is of the human possibility of recognizing in such realities the even greater reality of their interrelationship with man.

Adam was the first poet as he praised, by naming, those first creatures God brought him. Poets have been naming names ever since, in their human need to establish with the world exterior to them a humanly centered sense of relationship. Whether a poet's sense of relationships directly involves some concept of God is a matter of religious practice rather than of esthetics. But even the most self-assuredly agnostic poet practices what may be his unspoken and secular belief: that revelations (or meaningful recognitions) derive only from a sense of relationships.

It is with the relationships between image and idea that I am most immediately concerned, as those relationships between man and his world involve, in poetry, the complexities of metaphor and symbol. "Propeller," for instance, is a "symbolic poem" in that the literal marine propeller has come to stand (in my writing out my human sense of it) for *more* than it literally is. I've tried to confirm, by simple introductory description, what a reader's sense of a huge propeller might be. But only by metaphor (by "talking about one thing in terms of another") could I share with readers my sense of what more-than-itself the propeller symbolizes. Just as the image of a Cross may seem to various individuals to symbolize. "The Church," "Calvary," or "Christ," there is never a single, perfect, arithmetic equation between image and symbol. But if a poet has done his work well, he has so controlled his images and metaphors that the symbol can, and must, be read in terms of his own recognition of it.

Propeller

> Caged lightly by two-by-fours, rigged flat
> on a low-bed trailer, a bronze propeller
> sits stranded off Route 1. It almost
> fills both lanes: traffic stacks up
> behind it; and each car, passing, reflects   5
> its moment of the five blades' pure color.
>
> Honking won't move such a roadblock.
> Halfway, here, from its molten state,
> far inland, it waits an ocean: still
> to be keyed, then swung home, in a river dredged   10
> with old histories of launching and salvage.
> Incomplete though it is, and late,
>
> it will get there, somehow. Even
> as a huge tourist attraction, it cost
> too much to leave as part of civilization's   15
> roadside debris. It's curious, here,
> wondering at the magnitude of such work,
> to think how finally diminished
>
> the size will seem, in place, and of how
> submerged its ultimate function will be.   20
> But even now, as if geared to a far interior

impulse, it churns the flat light: as far
from here its cast will turn against time,
and turn dark, and it will move the sea.

"Propeller," then, is first of all about a literal marine propeller, an object of eternal reality big enough to fill two lanes of a major highway. But "Propeller" is also the product of my stunned response to this bronze wonder. And as the poem involves my human relationship with what I take to be a magnificent piece of human work, it involves (by definition and extension) the potential interrelationship of all men and all great human work. Any poet presumes greatly, of course, in assuming that *his* response is part of a universal response; but he could not write at all without such hope, and he must be judged not on his ego but on whether or not he has charged his images and ideas in a relationship his readers can meaningfully recognize.

"Propeller" is based on a simple enough, if unique, image. But *how* I talk about that image involves those questions of tone which can only be asked by the closest examination of the poem's language. The very first word of the poem, for instance, suggests that the propeller has some life of its own. Why, one might ask a student, wouldn't *crated* be better than *caged*? It obviously would, in terms of literal description. But *caged* is basically metaphorical: it talks about a propeller in terms of something more than a propeller and, in so doing, begins the poem by suggesting that the poet's attitude toward this propeller involves a uniquely human response. That this *caged* image is seen in line 3 as being *stranded* is, I hope, only further corroboration of my now analytic point.

What is this propeller, then, if it is both a propeller and *more* than a propeller? It is not *other than* a propeller (poets leave puzzles to puzzlers, as students might well be reminded); it is a propeller come to symbolize more than itself, as a human view of it involves a human relationship. Any marine architect might recognize that it is bronze, huge, colorful, inconveniently delayed, and incomplete. But as the poet writes out his recognition of that literal image, he fuses with literal recognition his sense (*caged, stranded*, and even *moment* —in the sense of both physics and history) that this propeller is seemingly organic, that its natural habitat is as eternal as the sea, and yet that it involves some concept of time.

No student should, of course, be *told* anything of the kind. But can't students be asked how *moment* (line 6) relates to *old histories* (line 11)? Can't students be brought to discover something of the ambivalence of experience by being asked why the poem claims that this propeller is *both* a *roadblock* (unmoved by suburban traffic) *and* a *tourist attraction*? And in what further sense can this propeller (now no longer merely literal) "cost / too much to leave as part of civilization's / roadside debris"?

How did *civilization* (line 15) get in here? And what does *civilization* have to do with "old histories of launching and salvage"? Why does one wonder at the "magnitude of such work" (line 17) and why—for that matter—does the poet abstract (in the course of the poem) from the specific "Propeller" of the title to the magnitude of *such work?* All such ways of talking about a propeller, and all such questions, involve the poet's attitude toward it. All such matters of his language are fused with his central image and can hardly be questioned separately.

But questioned they must be, in their full interrelationships, if whatever teacher, by his own attitude, is to demonstrate to students that the world is forever worth questioning. A poet questions the essential poetry of the world to discover for himself how his ideas relate to the world's thick images. He writes, I think, in hope of sharing how he *feels* the world, and he senses in that feeling his sense of relationship to it. No less, I think, can be asked of teachers, if they are to move students toward Frost's "Neither Out Far Nor In Deep," toward Yeats' "Among School Children," toward Stevens' "Sunday Morning," or toward whatever poems may answer the questions raised by their growing need.

PART FOUR

Approaching Poems

If there were panaceas for all the difficulties one encounters in teaching poetry, they would long ago have seen print. In education journals we find a miscellany of explications, ways of making poetry "alive" or meaningful for students (often written as "How-I-did-it" devices), and suggestions about what poems belong where in the curriculum—and why. Embedded in these writings are sound ideas and approaches; you will sometime translate or modify them and put them to excellent use in your classes.

More useful reading for some teachers-to-be lies in theoretical and analytical texts. Depending on your background, books such as William Martz' *Beginnings in Poetry,* or Perrine's *Sound and Sense,* or Ciardi's *How Does a Poem Mean?,* Brooks and Warren's *Understanding Poetry,* Friedman and McLaughlin's *Poetry: An Introduction to Its Form and Art,* or Elizabeth Drew's *Poetry: A Modern Guide to Its Understanding and Enjoyment* might generate so much light that your teaching of poetry will be forever bright.

But not all readers can manage the linguistic and conceptual abstraction of some of the books named above. Those who are unsure readers should schedule several hours each week for reading poetry. Nothing will substitute for such reading; both pleasure and instruction may develop. The unsure teacher might remember this golden rule: Refuse to substitute facts about poetry for the reading and considering of poems. Avoid, too, the enticements of your own definitive explication, the lures of abstract theoretical talk. Instead, prepare poems for teaching and then work through the poems with the students. Ask them questions you wouldn't mind answering yourself; avoid the quicksilver term until it has meaning for you.

Each of the following twelve problems raises one or more teaching issues; I have set these issues within the context of the junior and senior high. Consider the issues and the strategies suggested in each problem. Work out answers where they are called for. My hope here is to provoke thought and ideas rather than to provide models for emulation.

Problem 1: Defining poetry

Every English teacher with long mileage has been asked: "Of what *use* is poetry?" The last time I heard the question it was cast by an eleventh-grader (in a grey-flannel blazer) this way: "What *practical* good is it?" (The question was asked as though any answer not directly related to the Gross National Product would be challenged.)

I *might* sometimes try an unconvincing "Poetry can make you a better human being" on one kind of student, or a romantic "Poetry will enlarge your horizons" on another. To the serious student, I would cite the "What use is poetry?" chapter in Gilbert Highet's *The Powers of Poetry.* When I teach poetry well, of course, students don't ask about its value.

I'm more interested in trying to define poetry than in explaining its "uses." The question "What is poetry?" *is* worth some class time. If a student doesn't ask the question, you might. But a textbook or dictionary definition isn't worth going after. I hide behind Louis Armstrong. When asked to define *jazz*, he said, "If you have to ask what it is, nothing I say's gonna help."

It is often more important to ask a perplexing and involving question than to provide a neat answer. In any case, students should work out their own answers. Hold the "What is poetry?" question until you have taught many poems; consider it when you are ready to provide some of the materials from which answers can develop.

(An eighth-grade class.)
    TEACHER. I'm really not sure. What do you think poetry is?
    CARL. Flowery writing.
    MARY. It's usually about flowers or nature. Old things.
    TEACHER. But saying what it's about doesn't say what it is. Couldn't any kind of writing be flowery? Couldn't ordinary writing be about flowers or nature or—what did you say?—old things?

ANDY. It looks different than ordinary writing.

TEACHER. Always?

ANDY. Sure looks different to me. Always, I guess.

TEACHER. How?

ANDY. The way it's arranged.

EDITH. Poetry's put on the page different. It's in lines. And has rhyme and stuff.

TEACHER. Always has rhyme? What other stuff do you mean?

How poetry differs from prose is a start toward definition. It's easy enough to get students to look at poems with you and generalize the obvious differences: Most poetry "looks different" from prose; poetry tends to be heavy with images, most of them nonliteral (and therefore troublesome to literal-minded youngsters); poetry is usually condensed, tight utterance: "unimportant" (often syntax-setting) words are boiled out of many good poems. Students can see such characteristics, but seeing them isn't defining poetry. Back to the eighth-graders.

CARL. Why won't you define it? You ask *us* to define things.

TEACHER. I can tell you what the dictionary says. Poetry is defined in my desk dictionary as metrical writing. Another definition of poetry is this: the productions of a poet. Now are we settled on a definition?

(Silence.)

MARY. You mean anything a poet produces is poetry?

TEACHER. I'm not sure. Remember, those weren't my definitions.

CARL. They sure don't help much.

TEACHER. Let's try something other than dictionary definitions. *(On the chalkboard.)* "The marching band was a splash of sound and color." "Between classes the hallway is. . . ." Who will finish it?

ANDY. A riot.

EDITH. A mess.

BILL. The hallway is a can of live sardines.

TEACHER. That's a little gruesome, but nice. *(On chalkboard.)* "A poem is a wild flower in a haunted house." Now you try it "A poem is. . . ."

ANDY. Trouble.

EDITH. Pepper on a white table.

BILL. Ice cubes from a cool idea.

JOHN. A poem is conversation with an angel.

BILL. With a devil, you mean.

The metaphors wouldn't come this fast, nor would they define very precisely. On the other hand, they are more *interesting* definitions than Webster's.

Neither differences between poetry and prose nor the making of metaphor goes far enough. Older students might work toward definition from a sheet of markedly different poems. Poets have said what poetry is, and that might be a starting place for another class. For your wisest class, poems that say what a poem is (or what it is a poet tries to do) might serve. Barriss Mills' "Gone Forever" and Gregory Corso's "Poets Hitchhiking on the Highway" could be considered along with Charles Bukowski's "The Loser" (page 34). Such poems, relatively simple, might lead to Marianne Moore's "Poetry" and Archibald MacLeish's "Ars Poetica."

Problem 2: Toward meaning / Skeletons

Now that a definition for poetry has been properly negotiated (that is, cleverly avoided), a step toward getting the meaning of a poem is in order. I own a curriculum guide containing this suggestion about meaning: "Have students express the thought of a poem in one well-constructed sentence." Poets would snort at this suggestion. "What student can express the thought . . . ?" "There isn't a single thought in most poems, in the first place." "A poem means what it is." And so on.

But poets aside, for the moment, having students reduce a poem to skeleton statements *may* be a way of starting toward meaning. What the making of skeleton statements requires is the clearing of unknown words and allusions (sometimes through context-guessing) and an approximate (very loose) paraphrase. A skeleton does *not* require understanding of all ambiguity, a precise fix on the speaker or the tone, a consideration of all structural and formal elements. It is, then, a reduction of a poem's basic subject, theme, or "scene." A sentence or two will do for most poems. The reduction should stop just short of absurdity. A skeleton requires the student to prove that he has read carefully enough to know what's going on — in general. Skeletons provide the base for more particular talk. A serviceable skeleton statement is one that barely touches on particular figures and yet represents the main sense; serviceable skeletons are thus hard come by. With practice, however, students will achieve them.

(A twelfth-grade class.)

TEACHER. Some of the fun of writing a poem, then, is taking on the problems posed by fixed forms. You know some obvious things about sonnets—the line length, for example, the number of lines, the patterns for end rhymes, et cetera. Knowing these formal conventions is one thing; knowing what they mean to a poet who decides to follow them is another. Look at Sonnet 73 with me. Let's try to get past form to the the question of how form and idea work together. (*Read aloud as students follow in texts.*)

Sonnet 73

> That time of year thou mayst in me behold
> When yellow leaves, or none, or few, do hang
> Upon those boughs which shake against the cold,
> Bare ruin'd choirs where late the sweet birds sang.
> In me thou see'st the twilight of such day
> As after sunset fadeth in the west,
> Which by and by black night doth take away,
> Death's second self, that seals up all in rest.
> In me thou see'st the glowing of such fire
> That on the ashes of his youth doth lie,
> As the death-bed whereon it must expire,
> Consum'd with that which it was nourish'd by.
> This thou perceiv'st, which makes thy love more strong,
> To love that well which thou must leave ere long.
>
> WILLIAM SHAKESPEARE

TEACHER. Read the poem again silently. Then write out an answer to the question I put on the board. (*On chalkboard.*) "Write in one or two sentences what general meaning the poem has."

CARL. Do you mean paraphrase?

TEACHER. Not exactly. Don't take on the line-by-line meaning. "Summarize" is close to what I mean. Consider your answers a skeleton of the poem's meaning. . . .

MARY. How about this? It's fall. The yellow leaves —

ANDY. She'll never make it in two sentences!

TEACHER. Can you, Andy?

ANDY. Here's what I have, and it's only one fine sentence long. I'm getting old, my sun is setting, my fire's going out, so love me while you can.

TEACHER. That's closer to a summary, I think. You used particular images from the poem, though, so we'd have to accept your interpretation of those images if we are to accept your skeleton. Who else?

BILL. You see that I'm getting old. . . .

Thomas and Brown suggest this skeleton for Sonnet 73: "You know that I am growing old; therefore you love me more, since you must soon leave me."[1]

Unless something close to this skeleton emerges, you may be unwise to approach through Sonnet 73 such complex matters as the interrelations of form, the consideration of speaker, of diction, of the progressively more complex images. If students genuinely try but cannot produce a skeleton, the poem in question might better be set aside for study later. One useful check on a skeleton statement is whether it is general enough that students can imagine other poems treating the subject in prominently different ways. As Thomas and Brown say of their skeleton:

> In most poems (not in all) this plain sense meaning is of considerable importance; but it is never more than the skeleton of the experience. A person, as we see him, is not that particular person because of his bone-frame; his individuality, to us, is his whole appearance. So the plain sense of this poem might be the skeleton of a hundred poems, each different. The poem is itself unique, because of the flesh and blood (so to speak) on its skeleton — that is, the meaning of all the words working together as a whole.[2]

Why begin with skeleton or kernel statements rather than with total-poem paraphrase? Chiefly because it is difficult to move from paraphrase to broader considerations of form, idea, and language. Paraphrase, a time-honored, useful method of explication, tends to keep us from the whole poem. It focuses a tight scrutiny on particular images, single words, individual lines. Such scrutiny, capable of providing intense interest and excitement, is more profitably a late rather than an early step. Moreover, beginning the examination of a poem through paraphrase places the burden of paraphrase (and the authority for *correct* and *precise* restatement) on the teacher. This burden should properly be borne by students.

I don't mean to imply that a poem's meaning is up for grabs. We surely have the responsibility for knowing a poem as totally and wisely as we're able. But I take the teaching issue to be how I can

1. Wright Thomas and Stuart Gerry Brown, *Reading Poems: An Introduction to Critical Study* (New York: Oxford University Press, 1941), p. 744.
2. Thomas and Brown, p. 744.

best help students make their experience overlap with the experience in a poem. My paraphrase will not always help students make these approximations; indeed, my paraphrase will often relieve the student of the necessity for investigating the mysteries of *what* and *how.*

Paraphrase, then, rich, full paraphrase, should often be the final treatment we give a poem. Before paraphrase are the establishing of a general sense or skeleton, then the clearing of ambiguities, images, and allusions, then broad consideration of form and idea, decisions about the voices in the poem and the attitudes the voices express. Such a sequence will not take anything away from the final jelling that paraphrase can be; nor is such a sequence a substitution of partial for full paraphrase. The steps between skeleton and paraphrase will reflect *priorities*, will reflect what it is about the poem that the teacher thinks it necessary to consider. Subsequent paraphrase will place priorities in perspective.

Problem 3: Memorization/Choral reading

When I venture into teacher territory to talk poetry, a favorite question is "What about memorization?" More often than not, apparent questions are rhetorical; they hide quantitative assumptions. Teachers really wonder about *how much* memorization rather than whether it should be required. In a particularly cantankerous group the "question" begins, "I have students memorize 'Sea Fever,' Polonius' advice to Laertes, the 'To be or not to be' soliloquy, and one sonnet each from Shakespeare, Milton, and Keats."

Where memorizations are required, little harm is done if the teacher is friendly, the requirement modest, and the penalty for missing a line less than a failing grade. At the least, students should have genuine choice as to what they memorize in fulfillment of a requirement. Better are classrooms where memorization is encouraged rather than required or where there are options to memorization (such as arranging a poem for choral reading). I dare say *no* required memorizations because of what teachers tell me in defense of memorization: "It trains the mind" or "My students love it" or "Students will be glad they memorized when they're older" or "The lessons from poetry will stay with them always." Humbug!

A colleague, Carlton Wells, suggests a wise and attractive course. Teachers should develop their own repertoires, Professor Wells argues, and thus encourage student memorizations from the example they themselves set. Hearing Professor Wells speak Frost,

Browning, and Dickinson has encouraged many teachers to do just that.

Only teachers with photographic memories will memorize all the poems they teach. For you who find memorization hard, slow work, whose repertoires are limited and painfully built, this warning: The first reading-aloud of a poem may determine its fate with a particular class. Few of us can, without practice, read a poem aloud well. Reading aloud requires practice and thought. Some first readings should be given by students prepared for the occasion. You may know fellow teachers or lay citizens who read poetry well. They are an abundant natural resource; invite two or three such people in for readings during the school year.

Choral reading is often fun; it can be valuable fun. Moreover, it is a devious but reliable way of promoting memorization without attaching the odium of "requirement" to it. Rehearsing a poem several times as they prepare a choral reading, hearing the poem from others as they look at the poem on the page, students memorize in spite of themselves. Indeed, if the "conducting" is active and useful, students will want to watch the conductor and get free of the page. Again, there's a push toward memorization.

Three principles are basic to planning choral reading. First, the end of choral reading is student involvement and practice in interpretation, *not* public performance. Second, after students have done several choral readings based on available arrangements, they should make their own. Many anthologies provide arrangements of poems, but much of the benefit of choral reading comes from the close reading necessitated by the making of an arrangement. Third, there are elaborate systems of grouping voices for choral reading, but dividing a class into three kinds of voices—low, middle, and high (or dark, medium, and light)—will offer variety enough for a start. From these three groups solo voices can be drawn. Then all that's needed is a poem, and a teacher to count the stresses and give the downbeat.

The excerpt below, from Ethel Romig Fuller's "Haying," is strongly narrative, dramatic, and engaging: four characters deal with an issue touching on economic survival. Because it is direct and literal, students can easily arrange it for choral reading. You might have several groups of students arrange the poem, rehearse it, and present their several arrangements to the class. Which is the better arrangement? Why?

After you have read the poem, consider the questions that follow it. Which questions would help your students prepare a truly fine arrangement?

from *Haying*

    The supper bell was ringing as Neill strode—
A bucket of warm milk in either hand,
The cat and her five kittens at his heels—
Down through the yellow tansy from the barn,
Where Tod and I were washing in the trough— 5
We laid the pipe that summer from the hills—
And said, his weather eye cocked toward the south,
We're in for rain by morning. The wind has changed;
So we'll be finishing the hay tonight.
Tod lifted his black curly head from which 10
The bright drops splashed, and glared at Neill—
Aw, have a heart, he said. *I've worked enough*
For two farm hands today, and there's a dance
At Mary's Corners. Neill, I have a date . . .
The crickets fiddled in the dusty grass . . . 15
I looked away. What could a fellow do?
And Nancy'd promised she would go with me . . .
Neill turned and went on slowly to the house.
IIis shirt was stained across the back by sweat;
He looked dog-tired. We all were; we'd been up 20
And in the hay fields since before the dawn—
How endless-long the murky day had seemed!
How hot! And how the green deer-flies had stung!

    And then I was remembering the drought—
The dreadful years with scarce a drop of rain, 25
And Neill had almost lost Glenacres, and
Had shot his herd of starving blooded stock.
And we'd gone hungry too. *We'd better stand*
By Neill, I said. *A crop of hay means cash;*
And cash is mighty hard come by these days. 30
But Tod was mad—you couldn't blame him much—
Don't be a fool, he snapped. *Neill thinks because*
We're kids that he can run us. Then Maurine,
Neill's wife—she's kind of little-like and thin
From over-work and worry, but sure good 35
To Tod and me—we'd lived with her and Neill
Since Dad and Mother died—Maurine then called,
Your supper's hot and waiting. Better hurry, boys!
So when we'd wiped upon the roller-towel
Beside the kitchen door, we dragged our chairs 40

Up to the table where already Neill
Was eating. He piled our plates with new fried spuds,
Thick salt pork gravy, cobs of early corn
And passed the blue glass dish of fireweed honey—
We kept our hives far up the old hill-burn—   45
Hot biscuits, and sweet butter churned that day—
Our butter gets blue ribbons at the Fair—
And no one talked, till, belts let out a notch,
Our chairs tipped back against the wall, Neill said,
Be sports, you kids! Hay means more meals like this . . .   50

Maurine's blue eyes were pleading, *Go with him*—
Not even Tod could quite withstand that glance;
So like bull yearlings bunting at a fence,
We charged the telephone. Tod got there first.
When he'd called off his date, I rung up Nancy—   55
Nan's pretty as crab apple blossoms, and as slim
As any alder tree. She dances too
Like willows swaying in the April wind—
But Nancy Saunders comes of farmer-stock.
Next week, then, Karl, she said, *when haying's done.*

ETHEL ROMIG FULLER

Which lines are spoken by characters in the poem? Which character
speaks each bit of dialog? What is the name of the "I" speaker?
What is the relationship of the speaker to each of the other characters?

There are several "interrupters" or parentheses in "Haying."
The first of these makes up lines 2 and 3. Find all other interrupters
in the poem. What do these add to the poem? How would the poem
be different were they left out? How will you treat these interrupters in your arrangement?

Does the poem have end rhyme? What is the system of rhythm?
(The poem is cast in almost perfect blank verse.) Will the rhythmical
pattern affect the lines of dialog? How can you "use" the rhythm
that is there without letting it make the poem singsongy?

Before arranging the poem for choral reading, be sure that you
know what all the words mean and that the figures of speech are
clear to you. Do you know the meanings of *tansy, Glenacres, blooded,*
and *bunting*? Are the similes clear? Look especially at the six lines
beginning "So like bull yearlings. . . ." Do you find and understand other figures of speech? See, especially, "his weather eye
cocked" (line 7), "the crickets fiddled" (line 15), "he looked dog-
tired" (line 20), and "Maurine's blue eyes were pleading" (line 51).

And then, of course, there's the problem of arranging the poem. Care to try it?

Problem 4: Saying something poetically

There are two sure reasons for having students say something poetically. First, some students genuinely like writing poems. They like taking on and completing a "creative" job. Writing a poem seems (but seldom turns out to be) less formidable than other writing jobs. Some students welcome departures from ordinary composition assignments. And, of course, other students will write poems no matter what happens in school.

Second, the student who has wrestled seriously with the problem of saying something in poetic form will read poems better. The good reader knows that the good poet has spent more hours *finding* words than the reader will spend minutes *reading* them. Thus the good reader reads carefully and slowly. He rereads. His question is "What is there here that I'm not getting?" rather than "Why doesn't this guy say what he means?"

Students like writing poems, then. They become better readers from trying to write poems. How can you encourage them to use language as well as they're able?

Most often, you will begin with tasks far less grandiose than the composition of complete poems. Perhaps too low-level to qualify as "poetic" activity are word games like ghost, hink-pink, jotto, et cetera. An aging but ardent gamesman, I like games for filling in the brief corners of unscheduled class time. My favorite game, good for one minute or five, goes like this.

(*A ninth-grade class.*)

TEACHER. I'm thinking of a word and it rhymes with *freak.*

CARL. Is it an Arab chief?

TEACHER. No, it's not a *sheik.*

MARY. Is it a small river?

TEACHER. No, it's not a *creek.* (I can guess what part of the country you're from, Mary.)

ANDY. Is it the nose of a bird?

TEACHER. Is a beak a bird's nose? No, it's not a *beak*

EDITH. Does it mean slim and trim?

TEACHER (*pause while I try to wiggle off the hook*). No, it's not *chic.*

EDITH. I was thinking of another word—of something *smooth* or *polished.*

TEACHER. Yes, it's *sleek.*

When a secret word is defined, its "owner" confesses and passes the turn to the guesser. If the "owner" is stumped by a definition he cannot find a word for, he must yield his secret word and pass the turn to the guesser.

Here are other devices that may seem worth trying:

1. Put the first four lines of a limerick on the board and ask students to fashion a fifth line. After several minutes, have three or four students read their completed limericks.

2. Give students the first line or the first few words of a poem. Ask them to continue the poem for as many lines as they think necessary. Call on students for their poems; let them hear the poem from which you quoted.

3. Have interested students search out a half dozen images that reveal a given subject—images of animals or people in motion, images of night or dark, images of shivery cold or searing heat. Have one set of images put on the chalkboard. After discussing the images, ask students to imitate their pattern (form and syntax) in creating images of related subjects:

Images found	*Images to be created*
animals in motion	vehicles in motion; animals at rest
images of night or dark	images of daytime or brightness

4. Explain what an occasional poem is, how it has served the poets laureate of England and the "patronage" poets. Invite students to search the current social or political scene for a subject fit for an occasional poem. Suggest a "public" rather than a private poem; suggest that it may celebrate an occasion in almost any "tone of mind" from fun-poking to protest—ironically, seriously, humorously. Suggest closed couplets for students willing to try the games of meter and rhyme. As a preliminary-to-writing exercise, suggest particular occasions and ask students to describe the tones the occasions call for. (Poems that appeared after the death of President Kennedy might be instructive.)

5. Have students follow their in-class reading of a story (or *short* novel) with the small-group writing of a narrative poem based on the prose. A narrative poem of from twenty to forty lines might cover basic plot aspects of most short stories. Before students begin work, you could illustrate the prose-to-poetry writing job by first *telling* the story of a poem (such as Noyes' "The Highwayman") and then reading the poem. Younger students might, as an alternative, try to make a poem based on a single description in a story.

If the notion of a promoting poetic writing appeals to you, reread pages 30–32 for other suggestions on getting started.

Problem 5: Occasional teaching/Clusters

The "occasional" teaching of poetry is a proper substitute for the sustained unit on poetry. Occasional teaching of poetry means both the *seizing* of occasions and the *planning* of occasions. In the first case, you will capitalize upon a variety of opportunities: a season or holiday or grey day that needs a poem; a class discussion of a story that ties thematically to a poem you know; a significant world event that might gain perspective from a poem treating a similar event.

The greater the repertoire of poems you have to draw from, the greater the chance that you will encounter an appropriate occasion. Single poems are more likely to meet the impetus of a seized occasion; clusters of poems, each poem reinforcing the others or groups of poems providing comparison/contrast opportunities, may better fit the planned sequence of lessons you find occasion for.

In the second case, the planning of occasions, your year plan accommodates a sequence of lessons on poems. Anthologies will provide sequences and particular poems; coverage of certain forms of poetry and particular poets is sometimes stipulated by the syllabus—especially for the eleventh and twelfth grades. But occasional teaching implies teaching poems that reflect your taste, implies modifications of any curriculum through your judgments about what poems will work with particular classes. While searching for poems for your classes, you will develop a sequence of lessons that focuses on appropriate and progressively more complex aspects.

In order to seize the occasions that confront you, you will need many poems other than your legacies from college texts or what you find in school anthologies or in course outlines. You will cluster poems together so that similarities and differences among them are exploited in a class period or two.

Clusters can be arranged in many ways; the grouping principle need be valid only for a particular purpose. If you want juniors to arrive inductively at some understanding of the conventions of the sonnet, a cluster of sonnets will be necessary; if practice in identifying speakers in poems seems worth providing, poems that clearly reveal various voices will be the material to start with. There are almost limitless bases: One handful of poems represents a particular poet; variations on a given theme or subject, poems alike (or dramatically dissimilar) in form make up other sets; poems may be grouped for study of similar metaphors, for their uses of irony, and for similar narrative techniques. Ideally, groups of poems should show a progression toward difficulty and from emphases that are readily understood to emphases that are substantially demanding. Developing a precise statement about what is to be learned from each cluster will make such sequences possible.

August from My Desk

It is hot today, dry enough for cutting grain,
and I am drifting back to North Dakota
where butterflies are all gone brown with wheat dust.

And where some boy,
red-faced, sweating, chafed,
too young to be dying this way,
steers a laborious, self-propelled combine,
and dreams of cities, and blizzards —
and airplanes.

With the white silk scarf of his sleeve
he shines and shines his goggles,
he checks his meters, checks his flaps,
screams contact at his dreamless father,
and, engines roaring,
he pulls back the stick

and hurtles into the sun.

ROLAND FLINT

Kansas Boy

This Kansas boy who never saw the sea
Walks through the young corn rippling at his knee
As sailors walk; and when the grain grows higher
Watches the dark waves leap with greener fire
Than ever oceans hold. He follows ships,
Tasting the bitter spray upon his lips,
For in his blood up-stirs the salty ghost
Of one who sailed a storm-bound English coast.
Across wide fields he hears the sea winds crying,
Shouts at the crows — and dreams of white gulls flying.

RUTH LECHLITNER

(*A tenth-grade class, discussing the poems above.*)

TEACHER. In the second line of "August . . . ," then, the shift is both of place and of time. The speaker is remembering. He is, presumably, the red-faced boy of stanza two. Where is the speaker when he begins "drifting back"?

CARL. He's not in North Dakota. That's all you can be sure of.

MARY. The title suggests a big town. And he thinks of cities later on.

ANDY. He's as far from that farm as he can get.

TEACHER. Where is the Kansas boy?

ANDY. In the corn.

MARY. In the corn really, but off sailing somewhere in his mind.

TEACHER. Isn't he sailing the "storm-bound English coast"?

EDITH. The real sailor is his salty ghost ancestor. The boy's dreaming. The last line says so.

MARY. The crows he shouts at become the gulls in his dream.

TEACHER. The speaker in "August . . ." dreamed too, as a young boy. Where does it become clear what his dream is?

EDITH. The end of stanza two. He "dreams of cities."

BILL. But the last stanza is his big dream—getting off that combine and away from his dreamless father.

TEACHER. That seems right to me. I wonder if the speaker hasn't got what he dreamed about, though. As a boy he dreamed of cities; Mary said the title hints at a big city.

JOHN. But the city, if that's where he is, hasn't worked. When he's old and in the city, he dreams of his boyhood on the farm. "Drifting back" means dreaming. Dreaming of.

TEACHER. He didn't make it "into the sun"?

BILL. Not even close. But I don't think he'd be satisfied any-where.

TEACHER. What is alike about the dreams of the speaker of "August . . ." and the Kansas boy?

The concern with dreams shared by these poems provides a basis for discussing them together. Is the "glue" honest enough that pairing the poems makes sense? Your discussion won't go far before the integrity of the pairing will be tested pragmatically.

Pairing or grouping poems promotes close rather than loose reading. Students trying to prove or disprove a parallel or a differ-ence look hard into the poems being considered. The complicated question of tone or attitude, for example, might be approached through sets of ironic, impassioned, or exuberant poems. My expe-rience has been that sets of poems encourage discussion. If students have frequently been asked to consider several poems together, it might be provocative to give them a set of poems and let them decide what brings them together.

Problem 6: Against wrong notions

Students' stereotyped notions about poetry tend to keep them from it. Worse, persisting stereotypes disengage them once they've been led to it. Among the durable impressions, two stand out. One is that the subjects of poetry are sweet and lovely things, are noble and historic things; poems are either *very* serious (and uplifting) or darned silly. The other is that a select group of people know what good poetry is. They can explain the goodness of good poetry in convincing (but not perfectly understood) terms. Among the taste-makers are anthologists, teachers, and magazine editors.

Explicit plans for changing such notions are called for.

It will not do, however, to tell students that poems are about many things. Nor will it do to discuss with them the fact that taste is an issue in *your* class, at least, and that taste (preferences, visceral reactions) can be modified. Letting students learn the truth through experience might work.

One technique that works against both pernicious stereotypes is to involve students in the selection of poems. Many of the poems students study and discuss should be of their own selection. I mean, *literally*, having students search out poems for presentation or study. Modifications of natural and learned teacher behavior are implied: your natural inclination to select for study all the fine poems you know (and learned about in college); your thrust toward ruling out low orders of verse; your impetus toward controlling all materials studied in your classes. So be it. Modify.

If improving taste in poetry is a worthy objective, you must start with the taste (or lack of it) students exhibit, and seek improvement. This means helping youngsters become dissatisfied with what they "like"; it means giving them experiences with poetry that are more satisfying than those they arrange themselves.

Occasional teaching, too, will often use poems students find. They will need explicit instructions about the kind of occasion you intend to seize or plan. Fashion a sequence of three points concerning the form or figure you want to teach. Set students the job of finding poems that will allow you to develop those points. Sometimes, at least, student ingenuity regarding sources of teachable, susceptible poems will astound you. But warn them against tearing pages from anthologies found on library shelves!

Other times students should prepare *presentations* of poems. You should not always give them the poems they are to deal with. If winter occasions in you some thoughts of poetry, if a handful of wintry poems seem to promise fit subject matter for comparison and contrast, tell students something about indexes, give them routes to the libraries they have access to, and turn them loose.

A conventional but useful device is having students make anthologies of poems. An editorial committee can establish the principle that will order the anthology. For seventh- or eighth-grade students, different times of the year provide an adequate ordering principle. Types of poems order another anthology: the blues, haiku, and ballads. Or more conventional, more complex types. One fine student anthology was ordered by subjects. Students took on the finding of poems about certain things: Cars and Traffic; People Going Places; Friendly and Ferocious Beasts; et cetera. Another anthology of great breadth and some beauty was arranged by a student committee on the principle of complexity: the easiest poems (about whatever subject and in whatever form) came early in the book; the involved, complicated poems followed.

Students deserve to participate in the selection of poems for reading and for study. The facts that taste develops inductively and that poetry is about many things will be learned through participation. If other wrong ideas about poetry prevail (the common belief that all good poems rhyme, for example), you can arrange to have students learn otherwise. When students make collections of poems, they do a lot of hunting, reading, and considering of poetry. Taste, I think, might improve through such activity.

Problem 7: Reducing abstraction

Through our work in college and through the books we read, through the mere process of experiencing and the melancholy process of growing older, we grow in our ability to understand and to use abstract terms. We often have to test abstract terms repeatedly before feeling certain about using them: *form* and *tone*, *mood* and *theme* look simple but aren't. One of the hardest jobs in teaching poetry is to give young, inexperienced students control over the terms we use—and expect them to use. If they are to gain control over abstract terms, young students will need considerable concrete experience.

Many words used in this book are abstract: *form* has appeared often. At times it leaned toward the aspects of a poem that can be readily seen; at other times it suggested profound (and mysterious) inner workings that only poets and angels understand. Consider the matters of form below. Then look at Problem 9, page 86, and see what Robert Francis means by form.

Like clusters built on similar subject matters (cat poems, travel poems, fog poems), clusters built on external form are readily arranged. By external form I mean those aspects readily discernible to the eye and ear. Types of poems such as the sonnet, the ballad, and the blues have discernible shapes; their metrical and rhyme schemes are only slightly less apparent. A seventh-grade class might get its primer work on form through exposure to poems that use external shapes to enhance their effect.

John Updike's "Mirror" is pertinent here.

> When you look
> into a mirror
> it is not
> yourself you see,
> but a kind
> of apish error
> posed in fearful
> symmetry.

Poems in the shapes of their subjects might serve as model for a kind of poem students can write. Witness the crow and the tree in the poems below.

Absolutes

(From an ink painting by Seiho)

> black on white
> crow in snow
>   hunched
>   wet lump
> on brittle branch
> remembering warmth
> remembering corn
> miserable
> as life
> is
> black on white
>   GUSTAVE KEYSER

Fueled

>Fueled
>by a million
>man-made
>wings of fire —
>the rocket tore a tunnel
>through the sky —
>and everybody cheered.
>Fueled
>only by a thought from God —
>the seedling
>urged its way
>through thicknesses of black —
>and as it pierced
>the heavy ceiling of the soil —
>and launched itself
>up into outer space —
>no
>one
>even
>clapped.

>MARCIE HANS

Would "study" of such poems help pin down the abstraction *form?* Would they lead toward consideration of form in its more significant senses?

Let me try another example combining an abstract term and a principle. The term *persona* (or voice or speaker) is widely used currently; it remains an abstraction for many users. Abstraction is likely to be reduced through inductive teaching. Induction implies the examination of — and engagement in — many examples before conclusion or generalization is reached.

Some sense of persona might come out of the hard and continuing consideration of different examples. Begin with poems where the "I" speaker is clearly *not* the poet. Here's a poem that will interest some of your students.

Southbound on the Freeway

>A tourist came in from Orbitville,
>parked in the air, and said:

The creatures of this star
are made of metal and glass.

Through the transparent parts
you can see their guts.

Their feet are round and roll
on diagrams or long

measuring tapes, dark
with white lines.

They have four eyes.
The two in the back are red.

Sometimes you can see a five-eyed
one, with a red eye turning

on the top of his head.
He must be special—

the others respect him
and go slow

when he passes, winding
among them from behind.

They all hiss as they glide,
like inches, down the marked

tapes. Those soft shapes,
shadowy inside

the hard bodies—are they
their guts or their brains?

                              MAY SWENSON

Poems such as Swenson's, probed and well considered, will provide
a firm base for a first conclusion: The "I" in a poem is not necessarily the poet. Other poems will allow answers to more difficult
questions about the persona: the attitude or tone of voice of a
speaker can be inferred from how and what he speaks; differences
between speakers can be established (and poems like "Naming
of Parts," page 22, would serve); consider poems in which it is often

(wrongly) assumed the "I" is the poet (and Shakespeare's Sonnet 73, page 67, provides opportunity); the problem of persona in a poem that seems essentially voiceless (consider "Common Sense of the Crows," page 84) can—and ultimately should—be approached.

Inductive teaching will help reduce the abstraction of the principles and the terms we teach. If induction is properly claimed a superior teaching method, knowing what it means and considering how to use it is worth some effort.

Problem 8: First things first

One principle of learning says that learning occurs best when the sequence of facts, questions, and tasks is from simple to complex. A second principle is that more learning occurs when what is to be learned is set in context: that is, when relations among parts are established. (If you are disinclined to believe in learning in context, think back to a fact—what year Shakespeare was born, for example—or an idea—what a conceit is. Is either *separable* from other things you remember?)

As you systematize your teaching of poetry, both the principle of simple-to-complex and that of providing a context for what you are teaching will be useful. Your general teaching aim might be to provide pleasurable, worthwhile experience with poetry. Within that general objective you will need discrete activities that get at the form and the meaning of poetry. Questions of where to start and in what sequence to proceed remain.

A first step in approaching meaning is the setting of a kernel or skeleton statement. A skeleton may be an early preliminary to rich paraphrase. But before paraphrase can be thoroughly useful, many particular aspects of form and language might be considered. Need everything that a poem is be considered more or less simultaneously?

In an important sense, the answer is Yes. The reader who experiences a gestalt with a poem doesn't first consider basic meaning, then basic formal matters, then the question of the speaker's attitude, then the poet's ambiguities, his use of symbol, et cetera: Discrete elements work together in producing understanding for the careful, knowing reader. (It is the gestalt or insight that sometimes lets the fine oral interpretation of a poem succeed so well.)

The pedagogical problem that won't go away is that we can't teach all things at once. We must atomize, teach and reteach elements of a poem, make progress as we can from the consideration of separate things and the relating of separate things. Thus one might argue for the skeleton as a starting point toward meaning.

One might argue similarly for teaching matters of external form before considering the complicated question of what difference form makes to meaning. Need a young student see poems in different shapes before the externals of the sonnet make sense? Might he need to get a sense of how most sonnets operate externally before considering questions of the functions of form? Is there a simple-to-complex sequence in which skeleton statements and external aspects of form come before more complicated problems? For some students, at least, providing such a sequence would seem desirable.

Assume with me that students have looked at and speculated about poems (shaped in ways like those of Hans and Keyser) in which external form relates somehow to meaning.

Common Sense of the Crows

> Those fabled crows watched six
>   men go behind
> and five depart from one
>   stark hunter's blind,
> and then flew down from all
>   the bordering trees
>
> and so were blasted. Truth
>   is what one sees,
> but consequence is what
>   he fails to see.
> They studied character,
>   not quantity.
>
>   JUDSON JEROME

The Crows

> I shortcut home between Wade's tipsy shocks,
> And lookout crows alert in the bare elm
> Ask each other about this form that walks
> Stubbled mud they considered their own farm.
> They know there's death and loss where such shapes go.
> I have no gun—I even feel akin
> To these rude, lively birds. But to a crow
> Kinship means Crow, and I'm not of his clan.
>
> Off they flap to the wood with a hoarse curse,
> And though the landscape's greyer with them gone

I'm glad they're skeptics—someday someone else
Trudging these ruts may raise a sudden gun.
Distrust me, crow!—the not-as-crow-, the other.
Croak, 'Damn your eyes!', and call no man your brother.

LEAH BODINE DRAKE

(A ninth-grade class, discussing the poems above.)

TEACHER. I think you're right about "The Crows." The speaker feels more friendly toward the crows than he wants the crows to feel toward him. "Distrust me, crow!" he says. And in "Common Sense . . ." the blasted crows trusted what?

CARL. Human character?

MARY. They trusted the motives of the hunters. They didn't consider consequences of being wrong about the hunters.

ANDY. That's wrong. The crows' problem was that they couldn't count. They didn't trust men.

EDITH. The crows should have counted men instead of counting *on* men.

TEACHER. No pun intended?

EDITH. Pun intended.

TEACHER. Is there a moral in this fable? A lesson?

BILL. First things first.

JOHN. I think it's more: Consider the obvious. Or better: Don't overlook the obvious.

MARY. This poem only *seems* to teach lessons. The second sentence could be a lesson. "Truth is what you see but complications can't be seen." Or "Don't study character. Count." But why write a poem to say anything like that? I don't think the lesson is important. It's the joke about common sense, the lack of which gets the crows killed, and human common sense. We get blasted when we don't use common sense.

TEACHER. Can you apply the idea of common sense to "The Crows"?

MARY. The speaker says, Have it. Don't study character, crows. Don't trust man. He's not your brother. Or the speaker says you can't apply common sense to man.

TEACHER. Man and crow are of different clans.

ANDY. Yeah. What might be common sense to one clan doesn't fit the other.

TEACHER. But the speaker hints that he is in the crow's clan. Where?

BILL. "I even feel akin." Related.

TEACHER. Are there other "kinship" words? Find five or six.

I've tried to show that interesting and profitable discussion can occur even though no attention is first paid to external matters of form. I'm not saying that formal matters cannot provide answers to important questions.

But let me be explicit: How many readers read "The Crows" (and the dialog concerning it) without realizing the poem *is* a sonnet? A sharp teaching issue is suggested.

Many teachers teach external matters of form as though they constitute a valuable and separate subject matter that needs to be taught before poems can be read. What is taught about the sonnet is the length of the line, the predominant iambic foot, the number of lines, and the two basic versions of the sonnet form in English poetry. But the reason for learning such things lies in what form contributes to meaning. To oversimplify, knowing how the octave and the sestet function in "The Crows" will help the reader understand the poem. Should we first discuss the externals?

The way this conventional function will be learned is from close consideration of sonnets that make use of it. It will not be learned well separately.

Formal considerations will help unlock the meaning of "Common Sense of the Crows," too. Considering the voice or voices of each sentence is a starting place. What voice shifts are there? What assumptions can be made about the speaker of each sentence? What effect has the final feminine rhyme of *quantity* after the masculine rhyme pairs of *behind/blind* and *trees/sees?*

Were external matters of syntax and rhyme in your mind as you read and considered the poem? How did you learn (or how are you learning) about such things? How can you provide experience that will make matters of form *functional* to students—who can learn, God knows, that a sonnet has fourteen lines?

Problem 9: Toward inner form

In his essay Robert Francis wrote that the poet "would like all parts of his poem—words, lines, stanzas, thoughts, metaphors, rhythms—working in perfect harmony and cooperation. The interconnections and cooperations of all parts of a poem may be called its *form*, because the poem was *formed* by working out of all these relationships." The sensing of some of these relationships, Francis suggests, will increase the pleasure of reading poems.

I charge Robert Francis with being a poet. He would have us read poems as poets do. He persuades me, moreover, that a worthy ultimate aim for the student of poetry would be to sense the "harmonies" and "cooperations" among formal elements.

But for many students, including those for whom the act of reading remains formidable, matters of form (*how* a poem says) are secondary or even unrelated to meaning (*what* a poem says). A real dilemma. We want to teach important things about form, but the poems in which important formal things occur are often complex and difficult to grasp. Do we then select poems that, however pleasant or funny or communicative, are empty of real and complex ideas? Or do we take the finest poems, however difficult, and try to paraphrase before considering formal matters?

You will have to decide how to proceed toward form and idea. Is it foolish to have students consider *external* form? Simple formal things (such as how poems look, their stanza forms, how their sound systems work) may be unnecessary for the student who may eventually see poems in the terms Robert Francis suggests. Such simple things may never lead a less cerebral student toward genuine understanding of form. Are primer activities like those suggested earlier wasted or misguided effort? The question here should be seriously considered.

Robert Francis took me seriously when I sent him early drafts of materials intended to be primer exercises on form. Concerning how teachers might help students learn something significant about form, he wrote, "Only an outstanding example [of a poem] could make clear how much, how richly, how intricately, a poem may be interrelated and 'formed.'" In a later letter he provided me an example and an explication:

It is natural to think of the form of a poem as something external, such as its shape on the page or the pattern of lines and stanzas, for these are the things we first notice when we look at a poem. But in fine poetry the external is a true expression of the internal. A poet forms or shapes his very thought and feeling and attitude. Words, lines, stanzas are only the outer embodiment of this inner shaping.

Take Tennyson's little poem, "The Eagle."

He clasps the crag with crooked hands;
Close to the sun in lonely lands,
Ringed with the azure world, he stands.

The wrinkled sea beneath him crawls;
He watches from his mountain walls,
And like a thunderbolt he falls.

Here are two stanzas of three lines each; but you miss the point if you don't see that the two stanzas give us the eagle in two phases or flashes: (1) at rest, (2) in motion. The mere fact of two stanzas is unimportant and uninteresting; but what the two stanzas succeed in doing can be exciting, for they give us two distinct snapshots of the great bird.

Tennyson leaves no doubt that this is what he is aiming at. He gives each stanza equal weight. He ends each with parallel words: "he stands," "he falls." And he binds together each stanza with a single rhyme (*hands-lands-stands; crawls-walls-falls*).

This is not all. The boldness of the poem—consisting entirely of assertions (declarative sentences), and using short, vigorous words—what is this but a further way of expressing the boldness of the eagle himself? In other words, the poem tells us more about the eagle than the sentences in the poem add up to.

To make the texture tight and tense and so more expressive, Tennyson uses alliteration, *cl*'s and *cr*'s in the first stanza, *w*'s in the second. The "hands" are all the crookeder and the crag is all the craggier because of these interacting sound effects.

Clearly this poem has been *formed* from the inside out. Everything in it is part of its form or forming.

The least we might learn from Francis' close reading of "The Eagle" is how teachers might look at a poem before teaching it. The explication offers further help: Might not the *end* of instruction about form be the kind of precise reading Francis provides? Don't the abstractions need to be reduced to manageable terms before the "perfect harmony and cooperation" of parts become real to students? Shouldn't we stop teaching form as though it *were* simply a matter "of externals"?

Problem 10: Image and idea

"Image and idea are finally inseparable in a first-rate poem," Philip Booth says. Although there's not simple chronological sequence from image to idea (from feeling to thought), " 'image' precedes 'idea' for most poets as they write their best poems." Booth suggests that since a poem often becomes a poem *after* the poet explores his images thoroughly, the reader might begin with a poem's images and try to see how they interrelate.

The two "car" poems following offer good opportunities for considering image and idea both separately and together.

First Love

TO RICK

He serves her till his hair is full of grease;
He shapes her with love's fingers to his willing,
And talks of her alone, and will not cease
To sing her "mill," her "pots" — all his fulfilling   5
Is in her shining, snarling, patched-up form;
Her chrome and lacquer keep his spirits warm.

Not only that she's his, for he half-made her,
Or for the envy of the other guys,
He counts her worth the homage he has paid her;   10
Even the blast of pipes, to shock surprise
From quiet streets, and make the neighbors swear,
Not these alone explain his pride, his care.

The lash of cold wind through the wind-wing stinging,
The gold stab of her headlights through the night,   15
The scream of brakes — the gravel-spattered swinging
Around a corner, rocketing from sight.
By space, by speed, by danger drunk, beguiled;
Morning comes never, and the moon is wild.

EDITH MAY ALCOCK

The Flat

Calmly I step on the brakes,
grip the wheel with a firmness to choke a bear,
and ease to a stop,
my wife hiding her relief
behind a knew-you-could-do-it (but do-be-more-careful)   5
leer, the girls proud
of big-daddy protector,
complete with sitting-up-straight back
and neck of knowing. . . .

Afterwards, pumping the jack,   10
the kids chasing grasshoppers in the brush——
my turned-in eyes on a blowout at 95,
the lurch to the soft shoulder, jelly under the wheels,
over and over and over
flames/gas/bravery/failure/death   15

Now! dizzy with dooms promised,
this moment,
set for the worst,
ready to experience all-hell-let-loose,
expecting (in the sense   20
of pregnant) a horrible stillbirth;
I return to the bland safety of narrow escapes,
luck, and a God
to whom I have not yet become
altogether unnecessary.

LAURENCE LIEBERMAN

Images can be grouped under two general headings—literal
and nonliteral images. It would surprise most readers of poetry to
discover how few literal images there are in poetry. By literal I
mean concrete sensuous images: a thick, pale-yellow piece of pound
cake, its top baked brown. When teaching we often talk at length
about the five senses, about how our senses let us apprehend the
real world about us, about how our senses help us get into the
vicarious world of literature. It would be more to the point to consider how the senses help us into the world of figurative language.

Witness the poems above. Neither is flamboyantly nonliteral.
Yet it is hard to find a totally literal line in either poem: *serves* and
full are figurative in line 1 of "First Love"; *shapes, love's fingers,* and
to his willing are figurative in line 2; both *talks of her alone* and *will
not cease* are nonliteral in line 3. So with "The Flat." I find nonliteralness in each of the first 15 lines. (Agree?)

Two things account for the paucity of literal images in modern
poems. First, our language is richly figurative because man's things
and actions proliferate. Old words are used in new ways; most
added uses are nonliteral. New things men do require terms. Consider line 1 of "The Flat." It is easier to transfer *step* to the braking
operation (figuratively) than to invent and use a new word—say,
scronch. Moreover, humans like figurative language. Witness our
cliché-ridden language. Clichés are often metaphors dead from over-
exposure.

A second reason why poets rely heavily on figure is that literal
language lacks connotative richness. The poet needs connotations,
possibilities, ambiguities. This is what Booth implies when he says
that image precedes idea and that there is no poem until the poet
exhausts the figurative possibilities in his original images.

What value has such speculation for the teacher? It is possible to approach many poems through the question of the controlling image. Behind that controlling image a concrete, literal, real-world "something" can often be inferred. The concrete something started a poet thinking. What is inferred can be stated quite literally. From "First Love" I infer the sight of an adolescent working hard on his "heap." The poet considers the possibilities in the image. The boy certainly lavishes attention on that car. It's like a love affair. If I were that boy's girl. . . . The melancholy of the poet-speaker seems to tone down the exuberance of the images in "First Love." I can infer other real-world things—the hot-rodder's metaphoric vocabulary *(mill* and *pots),* the feel of his gravel-spattering cornering, the sound of his surprise-and-curse-producing throttle and muffler, et cetera. But my first inference is the key; it opens other inferences and gets me quickly to the figures that make the literal, real-world scene worth reading about.

Surely it's clear that my inferences hold no special prescience. Alcock's poem surely developed in ways totally alien to my inferences. But trying to get at the literal image behind her poem, considering how that image developed and picked up connotation, got me deeply into the poem.

The central literal image of "The Flat" is obvious. Beginning with that image, a scene most students can imagine (if they haven't been in it), the figures, ironies, rhythms, and meanings may be more profitably considered. What Booth calls the interrelations of images constitute the important meanings of "The Flat." But there may well have been an instant of experience that started this poem on its way. That instant may be a place to begin study. What happens to literal images when the intellect, the eye, and the ear get to work? The interrelations of images are worth considering.

Problem 11: Developing taste

Apple Peeler #1

Why the unbroken spiral, Virtuoso,
Like a trick sonnet in one long,
    versatile sentence?

Is it a pastime merely, this perfection,
For an old man, sharp knife, long night,
    long winter?

Or do your careful fingers move at the stir
Of unadmitted immemorial magic?

Solitaire. The ticking clock. The apple
Turning, turning as the round earth turns.

Apple Peeler #2

Why do you peel the apple, friend,
Letting its curl and redness around you bend?

A hobby is it? A pastime? Or more
A thing that needs doing to even the score?

Are your knowing fingers "wiser than 'ware"
Of magic and music, double foul or fair?

Red hands, yet guiltless. Apple yet
Answers to life's imperturbable threat.

Apple Peeler #3

Why the unbroken peel, Old Man,
Like a piece of spaghetti that hasn't
   been cooked?

Do your thinning fingers dance to the throb
Of primal immortal music?

Or is it boredom simply, your perfection,
For a Virtuoso, knife in hand, white
   night, long winter?

Back and forth, rocking, your ticking
   clock flowed
Down, turning as the round earth turns.

(An eleventh-grade class has read the "poems" above.)
    TEACHER. There's a TV game that ends just after the master of
ceremonies asks, "Will the real Napoleon Bonaparte stand up?" The
question you're to answer is "Will the real poem stand up?" Now
how. . . .
    CARL. Did you mean that pun? Will the real poem *stand up?*
    TEACHER. Hadn't thought of it. How about "Will the true poem
be revealed if we look hard enough and long enough at all three?"
    MARY. Did one person write all three?

TEACHER. The poet Robert Francis wrote one. The others were patched together by a timid soul who prefers to remain anonymous.

ANDY. Like you?

TEACHER. Like me. But I did the deed with Robert Francis' knowledge. He didn't *approve* my versions, you understand. Anyway, although there is only one "Apple Peeler" from a real poet, guessing which one isn't the point. *Determining* which is best is the point. So assume my questions to be honestly asked. The answer is less important than what goes into deciding on an answer. (*On chalkboard.*) Which is the superior poem? Why?

MARY. But that's a loaded question. You know the answer.

TEACHER. Work hard at answering the questions and I'll tell you which poem is Francis'. Fair?

MARY. I still think it's a loaded question.

TEACHER. You're probably right. Now get to work on my loaded question. Consider these additional questions if you're stuck for a place to start. Thirty minutes from now have your choice made plus six or eight sentences defending that choice. (*On chalkboard.*)

1. Can you rule out any poem for which you can't make a skeleton?

2. Has any of the poems incongruous (out-of-tone) words or images?

3. Can you find places where rhyme or meter dictates the choice of words?

4. In which poem is the scene laid out most effectively?

5. In which poem is the sequence or narrative most provocative?

6. Which has a speaker whose attitude is consistent?

I should first acknowledge Robert Francis' courtesy and apparently limitless good humor. And next I should make it perfectly clear that he is responsible for the true poem in the group above. What should emerge from the carnage is a method to be tested with students. Does the "diseased versions" device provoke enough close reading to justify its method?

I don't want to debate the issue of propriety. If the idea of altering a word or a line offends, find another method. Exercises like that involving "Apple Peeler" suggest themselves. Two poems describing identical subjects (sea gulls, city traffic, a hunting scene) can be compared. Which is the better (truer) description? Why? Poems of similar *theme* can be contrasted; similar metaphors in different poems invite comparison; poems of like mood, form, or even title may be considered side by side.

Let me meet one possible objection head on. Won't the *guessing* take priority over the *investigation*? My experience is that worry over the "right" answer soon disappears. Students sometimes become deeply enough involved that they forget to check for the "right" answer.

Wide experience with poetry is necessary before students are able to state, wisely and flatly, "That's a good (or a bad) poem." Students find the judging of prose comparatively (and deceptively) simple. Prose is familiar ground: the dialog, the characterization, the suspense of a story; the clear sentences, the thesis idea, the anecdote of an essay provide accessible bases for judging. Poetry is another case.

The main differences between prose and poetry are linguistic and formal. Developing a sense of these differences requires a great deal of reading and study of poetry. Your own efforts to involve students in the close reading will exercise your ingenuity fully. But since you hope to make the study of poetry pleasurable, since one of the great pleasures of reading a poem is the making of a certain, wise judgment, you will seek ways to promote close reading.

Whatever method you choose, the quality of performance is an issue to be settled through close reading. Taste, the ability to judge a poem, develops from being involved and from careful consideration; it does not develop from being told what is good or bad.

Problem 12: Teaching poems/An acid test

Although no poetry curriculum will guarantee the emotional and psychological well-being of all students, this book has proceeded from the assumptions that poetry can be made pleasurable, our teaching of it more effective, and students' involvement in poetry of benefit and use to them. From these assumptions, issues were raised and approaches to poems suggested. From the welter of issues and approaches, a final recommendation emerges: As you develop your teaching style and your convictions about poetry, plan lessons that embrace a variety of approaches.

The teacher whose oral interpretations are lively and dramatic, whose dramatic readings are surefire with students and personally exhilarating, should not fall into the trap of leading toward all poems from his strong suit. The same warning fits the consummate explicator, the compleat memorizer, *et al.* As Hook writes:

Francis' poem is (of course?) #1.

The solution [to helping students enjoy poetry] seems to lie in doing many things with poetry—not just one thing again and again. . . . Teachers and class can (1) read aloud, (2) dramatize, (3) present choral readings of, (4) sing, (5) discuss, (6) compare, (7) write about, (8) emulate or imitate, (9) illustrate with words, (10) illustrate with pictures, (11) listen to recordings of, (12) laugh about, (13) memorize (voluntarily), (14) collect favorite poems or passages, and (15) with modern poetry, serve as cocreator.[3]

You are ready, I think, for your final exam. You have been teased, angered, and cajoled into consideration of a variety of beliefs and suggestions. A fitting final activity from your reading of this book is the preparation of teaching plans for poems by poets Robert Francis and Philip Booth.

The ground rules must be clear. Read and consider the four poems on pages 96-98. Devise ways and means of presenting *two* of the poems to students of different capability and maturity. (You might want to make alternate plans for each poem, one plan using one approach toward a particular point, a second plan aimed at a different point and proceeding in an entirely different way. If you have access to students, trying out your strategies *should* prove irresistible.)

If you have no guinea pigs available, hypothesize a classroom situation—grade level, kinds of youngsters, what teaching has gone before, what things you will do later. You will find it helpful to write out the particular point(s) you want to teach. A sequence of steps will be necessary. You will plan the making of statements and the shaping of questions; you will arrange strategies that will involve students; you *may* want to construct an informal test designed to reveal whether you've had any success.

When a draft of your first plan is ready, check it against these questions:

1. What key thing did you set out to teach? Did you keep it in focus?

2. Are your questions—and the questions leading to questions —answerable? *Worth* answering? Do too many allow Yes-No answers? Are *why* and *how* and *show me* built in? Are there questions for different kinds of students?

3. Did you avoid the common pitfall of abstract "teacher talk"?

3. J. N. Hook, *The Teaching of High School English*, 3rd edition (New York: Ronald Press Co., 1965), p. 200.

Have you arranged examples that will make your abstractions manageable?

To put it another way, you will soon face a group of students. You will teach two of the poems below. Since you have some time to prepare for that splendid confrontation, get on with your plans.

Farm Boy After Summer

> A seated statue of himself he seems.
> A bronze slowness becomes him. Patently
> The page he contemplates he doesn't see.
>
> The lesson, the long lesson, has been summer.
> His mind holds summer as his skin holds sun.
> For once the homework, all of it, was done.
>
> What were the crops, where were the fiery fields
> Where for so many days so many hours
> The sun assaulted him with glittering showers?
>
> Expect a certain absence in his presence.
> Expect all winter long a summer scholar,
> For scarcely all its snows can cool that color.
>
> ROBERT FRANCIS

High Diver

> How deep is his duplicity who in a flash
> Passes from resting bird to flying bird to fish,
>
> Who momentarily is sculpture, then all motion,
> Speed and splash, then climbs again to contemplation.
>
> He is the archer who himself is bow and arrow.
> He is the upper-under-world-commuting hero.
>
> His downward going has the air of sacrifice
> To some dark seaweed-bearded seagod face to face.
>
> Or goddess. Rippling and responsive lies the water
> For him to contemplate, then powerfully to enter.
>
> ROBERT FRANCIS

Fisherman

Under hawk-watch
over the river,
quick-schooled minnows
riffle the shallow
where I wade.

Fingerlings rise
in the pooled jade
at amber flies,
but only
fish-hawk hover
or kingfisher eye
can see below
the current-run
and river-race
to the legend
lying dark
in slow-finned grace.

And I, who lost
the rainbow risen
in the torrent
of my need,
cast and cast
again where he
lies deep while
his torn gills bleed.

And the dreamer hawk
high over that pool
in the streaming air
cries high and cool.
PHILIP BOOTH

Sunday Climb

Over Holt's Ledge
the riding hawk slides down a ridge
of air; the hillwind blinds my tears
to his far flight, but the hunter's course
he cruises my mind's eye can see
down mountainside topography.

Set under me
in Spring relief, the green-mapped valley
tilts with every wing-banked turn:
the flyway, wood, and chicken run
are hawks' fair game from this blue height,
and none escape my hawk's high sight.

His knife wings part
the Northern air in neither sport
nor hate: he climbs the thermals, rides
downwind, as only his tightening
entrails ache. I barely escape
wishing myself a hawk's pure shape,

but under the stoop
of those talons my rabbit hope
lies small against the ledge. And I
climb both as killer and as prey:
twice alone on the last height,
the sheer edge of human sight.

                                        PHILIP BOOTH

PART FIVE

Poetry and the Library

The conventional literature anthology has become almost unmanageably huge. You've seen the omnibus anthology reviled in print; you've heard it deprecated in education courses. Is the three-pound, 750-page anthology a myth? Weigh one; check the pages.

But even such tomes, however well edited, hold but a thin sampling of the poems that might tempt adolescents, so uneven in reading ability, in teachability, in interests and sensibilities. Worse, even the newest anthology tends to be conservative rather than innovative. ("We put in those new things the teachers will let us!" protests one lachrymose salesman.) So far as poetry is concerned, adolescents characteristically respond to the innovative and resist the conservative.

The teacher, then, needs to go beyond the anthology for his poetry curriculum. The school library is his richest, most manageable, most obvious resource.

The classification scheme found in nearly all school libraries is the Dewey Decimal System. In it knowledge is divided into ten large categories, with the eighth, the "category of the 800's," assigned to literature. Dewey broke the classification down according to the various languages in which the authors did their writing. (A separate section is devoted to American literature as opposed to English, even though American writers use the English language. This is the major exception to the rule.) The 810's are devoted to American literature, the 820's to English literature, the 830's to German, and so on. Dewey further subdivided according to genres

or types of writing. Thus 811 is American poetry, 821 English poetry, etc. The same sequence is followed for other literary types,
with 812 standing for American drama and 822 English drama.

The books of any one category (such as the 811's, AMERICAN
POETRY) are actually shelved together in the library. However, all
the 811 index cards are not gathered together in the card catalog. To
use the card catalog a student must begin with subject, with author,
or with title.

The student looking for poems by American poets, for example,
will find the subject heading AMERICAN POETRY. This large classification, however, may have a lot more in it than the student wants to
find. More particular and direct use of the card catalog can be made
by the student who knows either the author whose poems he wants
to read or the title of a collection he wants to look at. The student
looking for poems by Walt Whitman or Ogden Nash can go to the
W's or the N's in the card catalog and discover what books by
Whitman or Nash the library owns. If he's after a particular collection, say Whitman's *Leaves of Grass* or Nash's *Parents Keep Out;
Elderly Poems for Youngerly Readers,* he can find the book under the *L*
or the *P.* The subject, author, and title indexes are, of course, all
arranged alphabetically.

But what of the student not yet persuaded that the card catalog
is useful? What if he learns, somehow, that the 811's are "where
American poetry is" and decides to wander by to see what's there?
Will he find everything the library has on Whitman's life? All judgments about Whitman by critics? The student may wonder, and
wonder he should.

The 811's will not reveal everything. Nor will a check of the W's
or N's in the card catalog yield the complete treasury of biographical
facts, of critical judgments, of writing by and about Whitman. The
teacher and the librarian must help students explore further.

One good way to explore is to go from the most *general* to the
most *specific* sources.[1] The general encyclopedia will tell the student
something about e. e. cummings. Encyclopedias frequently give
short biographies of poets, list their major works, and sometimes
offer the bonus of brief criticisms. Encyclopedias usually have
specialists write their articles; students will find a man of such
reputation as Joseph Wood Krutch writing the article on Edgar
Allan Poe. The general encyclopedias also contain useful articles on
the subject of poetry. The 1962 edition of *Compton's Pictured Encyclopedia,* for example, carries an essay on poetry by Stephen Vincent

1. See facsimile pages of selected reference works at the end of this part, page 104.

Benét. And the wise teacher and librarian know that certain encyclopedias are especially strong in certain areas: *Encyclopedia Americana*, for example, has long been noted for its excellent coverage in
the fields of literature and the fine arts.

At best, however, the general encyclopedia can give only a
superficial account; it is the place at which the search might begin,
but there it seldom should end. Among many special dictionaries
providing information about writers is *Twentieth Century Authors*.
Its easy, readable style makes it a natural for use with junior and
senior high school students.

Serious students wishing to dig deeper will find Spiller's *Literary History of the United States* useful and interesting. Most school
libraries will have additional (or other) historical-critical studies like
Spiller's. Some students, but only a few, should be led to the kinds
of information such books offer.

Students may want to compile their own personal poetry files
when they see teachers using theirs. Such files — arranged by subject, by poet, by tone, or by form — are worth encouraging. One student wants to read all the poetry of a favorite-of-the-moment
— James Weldon Johnson or Kenneth Fearing. Another wants to
make a file, say, of baseball poems. Still another asks whether anyone
writes poems about atomic bombs. Or a romantic sophomore girl
asks: "Has any modern American woman written any love sonnets
that compare to Elizabeth Barrett Browning's?" For these students,
an index to poetry is indispensable. The most useful, as well as
the most comprehensive, is *Granger's Index to Poetry*.

For the most recent writings by and about poets, the student
should consult *Readers' Guide to Periodical Literature*.

For both student and teacher, Brewtons' *Index to Children's
Poetry* is exceptionally useful. Teachers will certainly want to consult it when compiling their personal poetry files; students will
often locate there poems of immediate interest.

Literary, historical, and mythological allusions in poems cause
students many nagging difficulties. In order to understand the
classical poets (and, indeed, many of the moderns), students will
consult Benét's *Reader's Encyclopedia*. Here they will learn what
Milton means by "Stygian cave forlorn," whether Edwin Arlington
Robinson's "Tilbury Town" actually existed. In fact, students will
find much information in this handbook that will be helpful in
writing as well as in reading.

Sometimes a student will have a "favorite poem" he wants to
share with the class, but he remembers only a line or two from it.
Should it be the first line, the poetry indexes, such as *Granger's*,

will suffice. But sometimes the remembered line is not the first. Then the student consults one of the books of quotations. Because of its subject arrangement, Stevenson's *Home Book of Quotations* is a first choice here.

Many teachers, while teaching poetry, will make use of films, other visual materials (such as wall posters, slides, filmstrips), and recordings—both disk and tape. Here are two pieces of general counsel regarding such materials.

First, visit the library and find out what materials are there. Some school libraries are loaded with films, special materials files, and the like; some libraries, reflecting the trend toward making the school library the instructional center of the school, not only house instructional aids but provide listening rooms, viewing rooms, and study rooms. In other schools, what films and records are owned are stored in the principal's office or in the office of the chairman of English. The point is clear: Since audio-visual equipment varies dramatically in kind and amount from one school to the next, it behooves the new teacher to investigate the resources.

Once the exploration is underway, the second bit of general advice becomes important. *Go not into the classroom with film or record you haven't watched or listened to.* The consequences of the "unpreviewed" film are sometimes so grotesque or so unhappy that they should be left to the imagination rather than be laid bare here.

A good film, a fine reading, a wonderful slide may make the difference in the successful presentation of a poem. Checking what is available, discovering what can be purchased or rented for your use, and keeping an eye open for reviews and critiques of new audio-visual materials are among the things you will want to do. Students should learn from you that the classification and arrangement of the record and film catalogs are usually like those of the book catalog.

On the reference shelves of both school and public libraries are well-known anthologies of poetry: Palgrave's *Golden Treasury,* Untermeyer's *Treasury of Great Poems, English and American, et al.* Although they are often available as circulation books, some students will find them of forbidding bulk. Many excellent anthologies are available in paperback. At small cost, the teacher can have such collections as Untermeyer's *Pocket Book of Story Poems,* one of the several Oscar Williams collections, Speare's *Pocket Book of Verse,* *A Journey of Poems* (Dell), or *Contemporary American Poetry* (Penguin) as an integral part of his classroom. Nearly every library has a copy of the current *Paperbound Books in Print*; it is a handy tool for the teacher interested in building a poetry shelf for the classroom.

Anthologies? Only as a place to start. With the library close by, there is little reason to limit the teaching of poetry to poems collected in any one anthology.

Following are sample pages from eight of the reference books mentioned in this chapter, along with brief descriptions. The pages have been reduced in size, and some have been cropped. They are not reprinted here to give you factual information but to give you an idea of what the books look like and how they will be useful to you.

Encyclopedia Americana, Americana Corporation, 1962, vol. XXII, pp. 273, 274.

Twentieth Century Authors: First Supplement, ed. Stanley J. Kunitz, New York: H. W. Wilson Company, 1955, pp. 612, 613.

Literary History of the United States, ed. Robert E. Spiller *et al.*, revised edition, New York: The Macmillan Company, 1953, pp. 1157, 1335.

Granger's Index to Poetry, ed. William F. Bernhardt, 5th edition, New York: Columbia University Press, 1962, pp. 308, 1738, 2016.

Readers' Guide to Periodical Literature, semimonthly September to June, inclusive; monthly in July and August; cumulated periodically, New York: H. W. Wilson Company, March 1961– February 1963, pp. 1468, 1469.

Index to Children's Poetry: Second Supplement, comp. John E. and Sara W. Brewton, New York: H. W. Wilson Company, 1965, pp. xvii, 209.

The Reader's Encyclopedia, ed. William Rose Benét, 2nd edition, New York: Thomas Y. Crowell Company, 1965, p. 1006.

The Home Book of Quotations, ed. Burton Stevenson, 9th edition, New York: Dodd, Mead & Company, 1958, pp. 238, 2444.

Representative of encyclopedia articles about poets is this one written by Joseph Wood Krutch for *Encyclopedia Americana*. Essential biographical information about Edgar Allan Poe is given, as well as a listing and evaluation of the poet's major works. The poet's character and literary reputation are treated; an attempt is made to place him among the literary figures of his genera-

PODOPHYLLUM — POE   273

founder of the Soviet state, visited Podolsk several times before the Bolshevik Revolution of 1917 to meet anticzarist conspirators from Moscow and neighboring cities. The modern city contains a Lenin museum. Pop. (1959) 124,000.
                ELLSWORTH RAYMOND.

PODOPHYLLUM. See MANDRAKE.

POE, pō, **Edgar Allan,** American poet, critic, and short-story writer: b. Boston, Mass., Jan. 19, 1809; d. Baltimore, Md., Oct. 7, 1849. His parents were actors who were performing in Boston at the time of his birth. His father died, probably in 1810 or 1811, and his mother late in 1811, leaving three destitute children, of whom William died young and Rosalie ultimately lost her mind. Edgar was taken without formal adoption into the household of John Allan, a prosperous but childless tobacco merchant of Richmond, Va., whose wife seems to have been chiefly responsible for the arrangement. The handsome, moody, and intelligent child appears to have been treated with alternate indulgence and severity. He accompanied the Allans to England, where he was in school from 1815 until 1820, when the family returned to Richmond.

Edgar Allan Poe

The Bettmann Archive

    As he grew older, Edgar must have felt keenly his ambiguous position as nominally a member of a wealthy and more or less aristocratic family, who nevertheless enjoyed no security in that position. Endless controversy has raged concerning the extent to which Allan was responsible for the unpredictable and self-destructive behavior of his foster child. Allan quarreled with Poe after the latter was compelled to withdraw from the University of Virginia, where he had done well in at least some of his studies but had associated with a dissipated group and accumulated gambling debts which Allan refused to pay. Shortly thereafter, in 1827, Poe joined the Army as a common soldier. He had become a noncommissioned officer when Allan intervened to the extent of securing for him, in 1830, an appointment to West Point, from which he was expelled in 1831, apparently as a result of his own determination to be released. Allan now disowned him.
    In 1827 Poe had already published *Tamerlane and Other Poems,* a volume of no striking promise, and in the year of his expulsion from West Point another and better volume called simply *Poems.* Little is known of his life at this time, but in 1833 he was living in Baltimore with his father's widowed and poverty-stricken sister, Mrs. Maria Clemm, when he won a prize of $50 for his *MS Found in a Bottle* in a Baltimore *Satur-*

day Visiter short-story contest. Having thus attracted the attention of magazine editors, Poe spent most of his remaining years as a staff member of various magazines from which he usually either soon retired or was soon discharged as the result of erratic behavior provoked or exaggerated by periodic alcoholism. While employed successively by the *Southern Literary Messenger* of Richmond, the *Quarterly Review* of New York City, and *Graham's Magazine* of Philadelphia, he contributed poems, stories, critical articles, and book reviews which kept him barely afloat financially. They made him increasingly known, however, as the writer of sometimes acute but often vituperative criticism, of critical essays now recognized as the most original that had appeared in the United States, of poems marked by an easy but unforgettable rhythm, and of stories of which the best were always fantastic, weird, and obsessively concerned with death, decay, and madness.
    Continuing to live most of the time with Mrs. Clemm, Poe married his 13-year-old cousin, Virginia Clemm, in 1836. It has been remarked as significant that Virginia's pale beauty, fragile health, and childlike character seemed to embody the strange morbid ideal which almost from the beginning had been celebrated in his poems and stories. Of his devotion to her there has never been any doubt, and her lingering death in 1847 of a wasting disease seems to have hastened his total collapse. His alcoholism grew worse, probably complicated by drug taking, and he engaged in a series of rather absurd flirtations with minor literary ladies. His actions during his last few days have never been traced, but he was found dying at a Baltimore tavern in October 1849 and succumbed in a city hospital.
    Character.—The year following Poe's death the American journalist-critic Rufus Griswold wrote for the first collected edition of Poe's works a biography insisting so acrimoniously upon all of Poe's weaknesses that its intention appeared to be to assassinate its subject both as a man and as a writer. The controversy provoked has continued even down to today, and the character of no other American writer has been so hotly disputed. By some Poe has been judged almost as severely as Griswold judged him; by others he is pictured as the helpless victim of a crass society which persecuted the genius. The indisputable facts are that his life was a tragedy almost unrelieved except by such satisfactions as the consciousness of his powers may have afforded him, and that his weaknesses help to explain, if they do not justify, his treatment by contemporaries. His erratic behavior and general unreliability made him an unsatisfactory editor, while a certain arrogance and occasionally almost paranoid self-aggrandizement made his weaknesses even harder to accept. Yet there was a real element of heroism in his assumption of almost intolerable burdens, and there is probably some truth in each of the several explanations that have been offered for his failings.
    That Poe inherited a neurotic instability seems likely from the history of other members of his family, and that his treatment by Allan was unfortunate is evident. Heredity plus childhood trauma must have pushed him in the same direction, while the conditions of the journalistic world of his time made a career in it extremely difficult for anyone not capable of becoming an efficient hack. No other American writer so obviously invites investigation in the light of modern concepts

tion, his country, and the world. Cross references lead the reader to other articles in the encyclopedia which deal with the poet and with certain individual works. The bibliography at the end of the article lists other works concerned with the poet and his writings.

---

274   **POEL — POERIO**

of abnormal psychology; and while it is always dangerous to make detailed diagnoses on the basis of such fragmentary evidence as comes to us from the past, it seems safe to say that Poe was a genuine neurotic in certain describable respects. This was his misfortune; but it was also what made it possible for him to create a type of fiction superficially like that of the English fabricators of the "Gothic tale" which Horace Walpole's *Castle of Otranto* made popular, though different and vastly superior to these because, as Poe himself protested, his horrors were not contrived but genuinely "of the soul."

Literary Reputation.—Estimates of Poe's writings have varied almost as much as estimates of his character. Some have stressed the narrow range of effects he achieved in his stories with their unrelieved gloom, horror, and sense of impending disaster, their obsessive concern with death and decay. Others have been equally severe upon his poetry, which they have dismissed as melodramatic jingles whose popularity is due chiefly to an overinsistent rhythm. Even during his lifetime he was called by James Russell Lowell "three fifths pure genius and two fifths sheer fudge," and Ralph Waldo Emerson, in old age, remembered him only as "the jingle man." No writer is harder to explain in terms of the age in which he found himself, which is one of the reasons why his contemporaries found him difficult to accept. It was an age of the genteel, the wholesome, and the useful—three adjectives no one would apply to Poe's work. Yet the fact remains that Poe is one of the six or seven American writers of the 19th century who have won world popularity and worldwide critical acclaim. *The Raven* is probably the best-known poem ever written in the Western Hemisphere. Poe was an original critic, and he is probably credited with the invention of the ratiocinative detective copied by Sir Arthur Conan Doyle in England, by Émile Gaboriau in France, and by innumerable detective-story writers down to the present day.

Partly perhaps because of a different literary atmosphere, Poe's first and most ardent admirers among critics and men of letters were French rather than American, and it was they who did most to establish his international reputation. The French poet Charles Baudelaire credited him with having first revealed that "new shiver" which was to be exploited by the school of the so-called "decadents," and a generation later Stéphane Mallarmé recognized him as, similarly, a forerunner of the "symbolist" school which has tended to dominate French poetry for more than half a century. Even today many American critics seem unable to make up their minds about Poe. He is difficult to place or to judge by either conventional 19th century standards or by those of the highly intellectualized tradition of contemporary English and American poetry. Poe is almost completely *sui generis* and most original as the first great explorer the discoverer almost of those dark corners of the human mind where visions of unearthly beauty are mingled with emanations from that pit of the subconscious whence come nightmares tinged with madness. In fact, it might not be unjust to say that Poe was, among other things, the first of the surrealists.

See also AMERICAN LITERATURE—*3. The 19th Century* (Early Period): Edgar Allan Poe; SHORT STORY—*Craftsmen;* and separate articles

Bibliography.—Woodberry, George E., *The Life of Edgar Allan Poe, Personal and Literary,* rev. ed., 2 vols. (Boston 1909); Allen, Hervey, *Israfel; the Life and Times of Edgar Allan Poe* (Garden City, N.Y., 1926); Krutch, Joseph W., *Edgar Allan Poe: a Study in Genius* (New York 1926); Phillips, Mary E., *Edgar Allan Poe the Man,* 2 vols. (Philadelphia 1926); Damon, Samuel F., *Thomas Holley Chivers, Friend of Poe* (New York 1930); Quinn, Arthur H., *Edgar Allan Poe, a Critical Biography* (New York 1941); Winwar, Frances, *The Haunted Palace, a Life of Edgar Allan Poe* (New York 1959). The most complete edition is *The Complete Works of Edgar Allan Poe,* ed. by James A. Harrison, 17 vols. (New York 1902).

JOSEPH WOOD KRUTCH.

POEL, pōl, **William** (original surname POLE), English actor and theatrical manager: b. London, England, July 22, 1852; d. Putney, Dec. 13, 1934. He was attracted to the theater at an early age, having walked on with Tommaso Salvini when the great Italian actor came to London, and having been greatly impressed by the English comedian Charles J. Matthews, whose company he later joined. Poel reacted strongly against the scenic realism in Shakespeare which Sir Henry Irving had popularized at the Lyceum, and in 1893 he founded the Elizabethan Stage Society in order to demonstrate what he conceived to be the principles of Elizabethan stagecraft, presenting the plays without scenery and acted at a rapid pace. The productions he directed for the society during the 10 years of its existence were warmly praised by George Bernard Shaw, who was then dramatic critic on the *Saturday Review.* Among the English players that Poel brought to light were Edith Evans, who played Cressida for him in 1912, and Harley Granville-Barker, who was his Richard II in Shakespeare's play and his Edward II in Christopher Marlowe's.

Much of the doctrine in Granville-Barker's *Prefaces* was inspired by Poel's teaching, and to Poel more than anyone else the methods of Shakespearean production commonly accepted in the 20th century are due. His most famous production, however, and the only one to bring him financial profit, was his staging of the late medieval morality, *Everyman.* He also brought to life other neglected classics, such as Marlowe's *Doctor Faustus* and John Milton's *Samson Agonistes.* In 1927 Poel revived the Elizabethan Stage Society as the Elizabethan Stage Circle, and in the years following he demonstrated his principles afresh on a platform stage built out over the stalls of a London theater. This achieved the Elizabethan intimacy and space, as they have since been recovered in the theater at Stratford, Ontario, Canada. Poel was a pioneer who stuck to his convictions with fanatical intransigence, and actors did not always find him easy to work with. Nevertheless, he was a great teacher for those who could assimilate his methods. His visual sense was extremely acute, and his influence persists even among those who hardly remember his name. As an actor he was not remarkable. He published *Shakespeare in the Theatre* (1913) and *Notes on Some of William Poel's Stage Productions* (1933).

ROBERT W. SPEAIGHT.

POEMA DEL CID. See CID, THE.

POERIO, pō-â′ryō, **Carlo**, Italian patriot: b. Naples, Italy, Oct. 13, 1803; d. Florence, April 28, 1867. As a youth he followed his father Giuseppe into exile in Tuscany, France, and England,

Twentieth Century Authors, in its 1942 edition and its 1955 supplement, aims to give information about this century's writers (from all nations) whose books are familiar to readers of English. Articles, usually accompanied by a portrait, are a combination of information written by and about the author. This article about Phyllis McGinley characterizes the format: brief biography

MAC DONALD

Do Anything, 1950; Nancy and Plum, 1952; Onions in the Stew, 1955.

ABOUT: Current Biography 1946; Life March 18, 1946; New York Herald Tribune Book Review October 8, 1950; New York Times Book Review December 5, 1948; Publishers' Weekly March 17, 1951; Saturday Evening Post June 17, 1950; Saturday Review May 14, 1955.

MAC DONALD, PHILIP (189?-). For biographical sketch and list of earlier works and references, see TWENTIETH CENTURY AUTHORS, 1942.

* * *

Philip MacDonald has lived in the United States since 1931, working most of his time as a scenarist in the Hollywood studios. He is married and lives in Beverly Hills, in a house accessible only by hillside cable car, his publishers report. He has written few books in recent years, but his reputation as a detective story writer is still secure. Reviewing his *Something to Hide* in 1952, Anthony Boucher wrote: "MacDonald is at once a craftsman of writing, whose prose, characterization and evocation of mood (comic or terrible) might be envied by the most serious literary practitioner, and a craftsman of plot technique, whose construction and misdirection should delight (and startle) Carr or Christie."

ADDITIONAL WORKS: The Dark Wheel (with A. B. Correll) 1948; Something to Hide (short stories) 1952; Guest in the House, 1955.

MACDONELL, ARCHIBALD GOR-DON (November 3, 1895-January 16, 1941). For biographical sketch and list of works and references, see TWENTIETH CENTURY AUTHORS, 1942.

* * *

ADDITIONAL WORK: The Fur Coat (play) 1943.

MC FALL, Mrs. FRANCES ELIZA-BETH. See GRAND, S.

MACFALL, HALDANE (July 24, 1860-July 25, 1928). For biographical sketch and list of works and references, see TWENTIETH CENTURY AUTHORS, 1942.

MC FEE, WILLIAM (June 15, 1881-). For autobiographical sketch and list of earlier works and references, see TWENTIETH CENTURY AUTHORS, 1942.

* * *

In 1946 William McFee published his reminiscences of life aboard tramp steamers more than thirty years before, under the title

In the First Watch. "A rewarding book," Jennings Rice wrote of it, "deliberately unromantic in tone but filled with mellow wisdom and an honest nostalgia for days that are no more." McFee retired Chief Engineer Spenlove from the English merchant marine, but did not abandon him as a literary subject. He appears again, living quietly but not uneventfully in his English countryside home, in the novel *Family Trouble.* McFee himself lives in Roxbury, Conn.

ADDITIONAL WORKS: Ship to Shore, 1944; World's Great Tales of the Sea (ed.) 1944; In the First Watch (autobiography) 1946; Family Trouble, 1949; The Law of the Sea (non-fiction) 1950; The Adopted, 1952.

ABOUT: McFee, W. In the First Watch; Warfel, H. R. American Novelists of Today.

MC GINLEY, PHYLLIS (March 21, 1905-), American poet and author of children's books, was born in Ontario, Ore., the daughter of Daniel McGinley and Julia (Kiesel) McGinley; the family moved to Colorado and Utah when the author was very young. At one time Phyllis McGinley and her brother were the only pupils at a rural Colorado school. She was educated at the Sacred Heart Academy, Ogden, Utah, and attended the Universities of Utah and California. After teaching for one year in Utah, Miss McGinley went east to New York, on the strength of having sold several poems and having written an operetta for children. She held an assortment of odd jobs in New York, ranging from writing copy for an advertising agency and teaching school in New Rochelle to writing on the staff of *Town and Country.*

"I'd always written verse," she says, "since at the age of six I went introspective and turned out this little stunner:

> Sometimes in the evening
>   When the sky is red and pink
> I love to lie in a hammock
>   And think and think and think.

Which must be the beginning of my life-long preference for composing my stuff in a horizontal position."

Her first book was a volume of poems, *On the Contrary.* While they fell into the category of "light verse," said the New York *Times,* "she has instinctively grasped the fact that light verse, so called, must also suggest that modicum of truth which saves the poem followed by a listing of writings and a book and magazine bibliography. Students will find both the original edition and its supplement useful; there are many cross references to the 1942 edition in the 1955 supplement.

from mere buffoonery." Several other collections of poems followed.

"A warm heart, an observant eye, a witty style and an open mind constitute excellent equipment for a poet," notes the New York *Times;* and *Time* remarks that her work "in praise of normal things . . . is disarmingly pleasant." Much of her verse appears first in the *New Yorker.*

In 1944 Miss McGinley made her debut as a children's writer with *The Horse Who Lived Upstairs.* Many others followed, including her alphabet-in-rhyme *All Around the Town* and *Make-Believe Twins,* informal verses arranged typographically as prose.

Of herself she has said: "My eccentricities are few—putting sugar in my soup is the only one I can think of at the moment—and I'm what is known in the trade as a 'good, reliable worker.' That is, I always make a deadline. I am not very prolific and labor painstakingly over every piece I do." In 1937 she married Charles Hayden and they live in Larchmont, N.Y., with their two daughters. In 1948 she wrote lyrics for a revue called *Small Wonder,* and she wrote the film narration for *The Emperor's Nightingale,* a movie of 1951. In 1955 she was elected to the National Academy of Arts and Letters.

PRINCIPAL WORKS: On the Contrary, 1934; One More Manhattan, 1937; A Pocketful of Wry, 1940; Husbands Are Difficult, 1941; The Horse Who Lived Upstairs, 1944; The Plain Princess, 1945; Stones from a Glass House, 1946; All Around the Town 1948; The Most Wonderful Doll in the World, 1950; Blunderbus, 1951; The Horse Who Had His Picture in the Paper, 1951; A Short Walk from the Station, 1951; The Make-Believe Twins, 1953; The Love Letters of Phyllis McGinley, 1954.

ABOUT: Kunitz, S. J. & Haycraft, H. Junior Book of Authors; Current Biography 1941; New York Herald Tribune Book Review December 16, 1951, October 24, 1954; New York Times Book Review December 9, 1951; Saturday Review September 18, 1954; Scholastic September 29, 1947.

MAC GRATH, HAROLD (September 4, 1871-October 30, 1932). For biographical sketch and list of works and references, see TWENTIETH CENTURY AUTHORS, 1942.

*MACHEN, ARTHUR (March 3, 1863-December 15, 1947). For biographical sketch and list of earlier works and references, see TWENTIETH CENTURY AUTHORS, 1942.

* * *

Arthur Machen died in a nursing home at Beaconsfield, England, at eighty-four.

* măk′ĕn

Living quietly in the country for the last fourteen yars of his life, Machen had done no creative writing for many years. In 1943 a committee which included Bernard Shaw, Max Beerbohm, and T. S. Eliot was formed to help ease his straitened circumstances.

Far Off Things and *Things Near and Far* have been called by J. M. Cohen "one of the best pieces of autobiographical writing of the century." Philip Van Doren Stern pointed out that a taste for Machen's elaborate and polished style, subtle thinking, and rich imagery must be acquired. His art, said Stern, "is firmly based on the belief that the mystical interpretation of life is the only one worth holding. Machen is the artist of wonder, the seeker for something beyond life and outside of time, the late-born disciple of early Christianity who sees the physical world as the outer covering of a glowing inner core that may someday be revealed."

ADDITIONAL WORKS: Handy Dickens: Selections from the Works of Charles Dickens (ed.) 1941.

ABOUT: Gekle, W. F. Arthur Machen, Weaver of Fantasy; Atlantic Monthly May 1947; London Times December 16, 1947; New York Times December 16, 1947; Saturday Review of Literature March 20, 1943; Spectator July 20, 1951.

MC HUGH, VINCENT (December 23, 1904-). For autobiographical sketch and list of earlier works and references, see TWENTIETH CENTURY AUTHORS, 1942.

* * *

Vincent McHugh writes: "I worked for the *New Yorker,* writing non-fiction shorts and an occasional lead book review, until the summer of 1943. I continued to teach the Technique of the Novel and other courses in the Division of General Education at New York University until the end of 1943. During some of this period, from late 1942 until August 1943, when it was dissolved by congressional action, I worked as a writer-director for the Office of War Information, Bureau of Domestic Motion Pictures, writing the narration and in some cases directing such pictures as *Mission Accomplished, Day of Battle, 4F, Soldier from the Tropics,* and *Caribbean Patrol.* I also did odd jobs—some of them very odd indeed—for the Writers' War Board.

"In the summer of 1943 my novel *I Am Thinking of My Darling* was published. The book was leased to RKO Pictures, and in the spring of 1944 I went to Hollywood as a contract writer for Paramount Pictures, where I did additional dialogue for the

The arrangement of Spiller's *Literary History of the United States* is chronological. Chapters deal with literature and culture, movements and influences, individual authors. Among the outstanding contributors to this work are historians Henry Steele Commager and Merle Curti and such literary figures as Henry Seidel Canby, Carl Sandburg, and Carl Van Doren. This scholarly

69. EDWIN ARLINGTON ROBINSON

THE quiet, straightforward speech in Edwin Arlington Robinson's keynote book, *The Children of the Night* (1897), was first heard amid a babel of other poetic tongues both old and new. Here were the simple words of a great poet, inaudible among bold voices: those of the humanitarian singers, like Edwin Markham in *The Man with the Hoe, and Other Poems* (1899); those of the new naturalists in poetry, like Stephen Crane in *War Is Kind* (1899); or those of the intellectual nationalists in verse, like William Vaughn Moody in "An Ode in Time of Hesitation" (1900). Insistent, too, reverberated the many special accents, the songs of the Western farms (Hamlin Garland and James Whitcomb Riley); songs born of learning in the seventeenth century (Louise Imogen Guiney and Lizette Reese); and, still influential, the Victorian melodies of Gilder, Aldrich, and Stedman, all of whom published collections of their poetry not long after the stillborn *Children of the Night.*

That Robinson approved or disapproved of these "movements," no evidence exists. Nor had he convictions concerning the other cults whose creeds until his death beat against his independent mind, sometimes repudiating his techniques and themes, sometimes claiming both as their very own. He remained quiet, he went his lonely way. Denounce him the innovators could, for he never sloughed off the time-honored forms of the past; claim him they could, for though indifferent to group ideas he had discovered for himself principles dear to imagist or expressionist. To a few individuals he was in debt (as to a few great writers of the past): to Ridgely Torrence, dramatist and poet; perhaps to Richard Hovey, for his American pioneering in Arthurian legend; and to Moody for confirming in him his passion for poetic drama. But in his aloof dedication to poetry he was singularly unaffected by the tides of contemporary criticism discussed in the last chapter. Unlike Babbitt and most of the other controversialists who wrote about criticism without much practicing it, or about literature as an illustration of theory, he was solely interested in the creation of literature itself as an expression of his own soul.

Among the poets whose influence he seems to have felt, William Vaughn work is most useful for serious students and good readers. The work's major shortcoming is the too brief index for so comprehensive a volume. Students who have access to a metropolitan or university library may find the separate bibliography volume helpful.

79. POETRY

AMERICAN poetry in these years furnished the most serious evidence of a cleavage between what we have learned to call mass civilization and minority culture. Ignored for the most part by the large number of readers who hearkened to the novelists and playwrights, there were nevertheless more expert practitioners of the craft of verse during the twenty-five years before 1940 than during any other generation in our history. If we accept the proposition advanced by one of them, "Artists are the antennae of the race," the most sensitive registers of our spiritual and social well-being or malaise, we cannot ignore the poets' evidence, even though much of it may be disturbing. Indeed, in the view of the most influential poet of the 1920's, T. S. Eliot, one characteristic of authentic poetry, whether by Blake or by Æschylus, "is merely a peculiar honesty, which, in a world too frightened to be honest, is peculiarly terrifying."

Eliot's own career raises at once many of the most controversial issues. In some accounts of American literature he is omitted altogether on the ground that he lived in England during most of his maturity and became a British subject in 1927. Yet his work can no more be divorced from its American background than that of Henry James; and at a time when many European artists—including W. H. Auden, the leading English poet of his generation—are becoming American citizens, we must recognize that much of the future of art can only be international. Almost as controversial, however, is the value of Eliot's work, regardless of what country it belongs to. By 1940 he had already lived through two cycles of taste. In the early 1920's he was hailed as a revolutionary by the young survivors of the war, by "the lost generation" who read in him their feeling of the breakdown of tradition and their sense of being thereby liberated, if only into despair. But when he found his way out of the pit inhabited by "the hollow men" by means of a return to formal religion, he was dismissed by many of his followers as a reactionary. Yet his preoccupations, from first to last, show a singular consistency.

2

Before we can see his career in any perspective we must reckon with that of the craftsman to whom he dedicated *The Waste Land,* calling him, in

FAME (*continued*)
  Perry Zoll. *Fr.* Spoon River Anthology. Masters.
  Pillar of Fame, The. Herrick.
  Public Acclaim. Hölderlin, *tr. fr. German by* Flores.
  Stanzas Written on the Road between Florence and Pisa. Byron.
  Substance, Shadow, and Spirit. T'ao Ch'ien, *tr. fr. Chinese by* Waley.
  To an Athlete Dying Young. A. E. Housman.
  Two Sonnets on Fame. Keats.
  Whilst thus my pen strives to eternize thee. *Fr.* Idea. Drayton.
  Wrestler, The. George, *tr. fr. German by* Luke.
  You that do search for every purling spring. *Fr.* Astrophel and Stella. Sidney.
FAMILY LIFE
  Autobiographical. A. M. Klein.
  Cotter's Saturday Night, The. Burns.
  Family, The. Lydston.
  Family, The. *Unknown, tr. fr. German by* Fyleman.
  Family Court. Nash.
  Family Meeting, The. Sprague.
  Folded Flock, The. Wilfrid Meynell.
  From a Childhood. Rilke, *tr. fr. German by* MacIntyre.
  Love between Brothers and Sisters. Watts.
FAMINE
  Famine Year, The. Lady Wilde.
  Song of the Times. Adler, *tr. fr. Yiddish by* Betsky.
FARMER, GEORGE. Ballad for a Boy, A. Cory.
FARMING AND FARMERS
  Agriculture; a Poem, *sel.* ("See where the farmer"). Dodsley.
  Canadian Farmer. Bartole.
  City Wife. Livesay.
  Code, The. Robert Frost.
  Country Summer. Léonie Adams.
  Crafty Farmer, The. *Unknown.*
  Day at the Farm, A. "L. J."
  Death of the Hired Man, The. Robert Frost.
  Defeated Farmer. Mark Van Doren.
  Digression from Husbandry to a Point or Two of Huswifery, A. Tusser.
  Drinking Time. O'Sullivan.
  Evening at the Farm. Trowbridge.
  Farewell to the Farm. R. L. Stevenson.

  Ranchers. Lesemann.
  Reaper, The. L. H. Allen.
  Rival, The. S. T. Warner.
  Seed. Bosman.
  September. Tusser.
  Sharecropper. Stewart Atkins.
  Sheep-Washing, The. *Fr.* The Seasons: Summer. James Thomson.
  Soldiers of the Plough, The. *Fr.* The Happy Harvesters. Charles Sangster.
  Somerset Farmer, The. Marguerite Wilkinson.
  Sower, The. Figueroa, *tr. fr. Spanish by* Fitts.
  Sower, The. Sir C. G. D. Roberts.
  Sower and His Seed, The. Lecky.
  Sower's Song, The. Carlyle.
  Sowing. Edward Thomas.
  Sowing Season. Hugo, *tr. fr. French by* Conder.
  Steel Glass, The, *sel.* ("Behold him, priests, and though he stink of sweat"). Gascoigne.
  Testament of Beauty, The, *sel.* ("How was November's melancholy endear'd to me"). Robert Bridges.
  Times Have Altered, The. *Unknown.*
  Watching the Reapers. Po Chü-i, *tr. fr. Chinese by* Waley.
  See also FIELDS AND PASTURES
FARRAGUT, DAVID GLASGOW
  David Glasgow Farragut. Wallace Rice.
  Farragut. W. T. Meredith.
  River Fight, The. Brownell.
  Through Fire in Mobile Bay. *At. to* Farragut.
FATE
  As I Gird On for Fighting. Housman.
  At the Crossroads. Hovey.
  Dice Were Loaded, The. Mary Gilmore.
  Eros Turannos. E. A. Robinson.
  Fate. L. J. Block.
  Fate. J. F. Cooper.
  Fate. Emerson.
  Fate. Harte.
  Fate. Ibn Abdun, *tr. fr. Arabic by* Arberry.
  Fate. Morgenstern, *tr. fr. German by* Hull.
  Fate. S. M. Spalding.
  Genseric. "Owen Meredith."
  Hap. Hardy.
  Hymn to Chance. H. P. Putnam.
  Inevitable, The. S. K. Bolton.

Granger's Index to Poetry, now in its fifth edition, is divided into three parts. Part I is a title and first-line index; Part II is an author index; and Part III is a subject index, all arranged alphabetically. This edition, like its predecessors, is a large, heavy volume set in small print. Some students will need help in using the book; all should be encouraged to read the book's preface, explanatory notes, and key to symbols. The fifth edition indexes 574 anthologies, including 110 new titles. The subject index has been expanded from previous editions. Holidays, seasons, famous persons (poems about Columbus, for example) are included.

Twenty year watershed program. O. L. Onstott. Il Am City 76:104-5 Mr '61

POCHETTE. See Violin

POCKELS, F.
Amateur scientist. H. Jaffe and J. Stephany. Il Sci Am 207:156-8+ Jl '62

POCKET billiards. See Billiards

POCOCK, Bryant W.
Slides to the rescue! Pop Phot 49:102+ S '61

PODESTÁ, Cata
Seashell; story. Américas 14:25-30 Ap '62

PODGORNII, Nikolai Viktorovich
Sharks, bureaucrats & dark horses. por Time 79:19 Je 29 '62

PODIATRISTS. See Chiropodists

PODIATRY. See Chiropody

PODOCORYNE carnea. See Hydra (zoology)

PODOPHYLLUM peltatum. See May-apples

POE, Edgar Allan
Three Sundays in a week; dramatization. See Nolan, P. T.
about
Principle of composition. K. Burke. Poetry 99:46-53 O '61

POECILIIDAE
Egg retention: pattern in evolution. D. E. Rosen. Il Natur Hist 71:46-53 D '62

POET in the paint store; story. See Saks, S.

POETIC imagination. See Imagination

POETICAL criticism. See Literary criticism

POETICS
Advice to beginning poets. E. Wood. Writer 75:18-19 Ag '62
Armenian heresy. J. Ciardi. Sat R 45:27 Ja 27 '62
Five thousand poems ago; writing light verse. R. Armour. Writer 74:15-17 O '61
Methods and the man. G. H. Hartman. Poetry 98:332-6 Ag '61
Poetry and luck. J. Ciardi. Sat R 44:39 O 21 '61
Poetry, and those difficult green years. N. B. Olson. Writer 75:19-21 S '62
Poetry column. M. Lineweaver. See issues of Writer
Poetry workshop. J. Holmes. Writer 75:22-4+ Ja; 21-3 Mr; 17-19 My; 19-21+ Jl '62
Poetry workshop. M. W. Kumin. Writer 75:22-4+ Ja; 21-3 Mr; 17-19 My; 19-21+ Jl; 16-18+ N '62; 76:21-4 Ja '63
Poet's letter to a beginner. M. Sarton. Writer 75:19-21+ Ap '62
Poet's preface; with poems by English school boys. P. K. Dufault. Horn Bk 37:127-30 Ap '61
Principle of composition. K. Burke. Poetry 99:46-53 O '61
Service to the muse. R. Graves. Atlan 207:43-8 Je '61
Ten rules for poets. E. P. LaSelle. Writer 74:18-20 Je '61
Write me a verse; excerpts from Take sky. D. McCord. Horn Bk 38:396-400 Ag '62

POETKER, Frances (Jones)
Trouble shooter for weddings. il pors Sat Eve Post 234:32+ D 2 '61

POETRY
Are you illiterate about modern poetry? J. Simon. Vogue 138:124-5+ N 1 '61
Between prose and verse. R. Frost. Atlan 209:51-4 Ja '62
Estate of poetry. by E. Muir. Review Sat R 45:20 Je 30 '62. D. G. Hoffman
For a wider view of poetry. S. Spender. il Sat R 45:19-21+ My 19 '62
From the bourgeois poet. K. Shapiro. Poetry 101:115-21 O '62
Letter to Karl Shapiro; with reply and rejoinder. R. Whittemore. Poetry 98:168-85 Je '61

30:11-15 S '61
Poet on his poem. P. Engle and J. Langland. Sat R 45:12+ Ag 11 '62
Poetry and experience. by A. MacLeish. Review Nation 192:308-9 Ap 8 '61. R. Eberhart
Poetry 99:191-4 Jl '61. S. F. Morse
Poetry and salesmanship. J. Ciardi. Sat R 46:22 Ja 5 '63
Poetry and such. H. Kenner. Nat R 11:417 D 16 '61
Poetry as knowledge. J. Ciardi. Sat R 44:8-10+ Jl 22 '61
Poetry in an age of expansion. R. Bly. Nation 192:350-4 Ap 22 '61
Poetry in English: 1945-62. Il Time 79:92-4+ Mr 9 '62
Poetry thinking about itself. S. Burnshaw. Poetry 99:387-90 Mr '62
Poetry to tell a story. W. Gibson. Nation 192:396-8 My 6 '61
Poets on the New frontier. B. Richart. Commonweal 74:175-6 My 12 '61
Questions and answers on light verse. R. Armour. Writer 75:39-41 Ap '62
Self-revelation in the new poetry. P. Davison. Atlan 208:170-2+ N '61
Talking points; concerning the response to Americans: a portrait in verses. J. Wakeman. Wilson Lib Bul 37:174+ O '62
Today's poet. W. H. Auden. Mlle 54:187 Ap '62
Trial of a poet. J. Ciardi. Sat R 45:14+ O 20 '62

See also
Childrens poems (by children)
Childrens poetry
Christmas poetry
Epic poetry
Parnassians
Parody
Poetics
Poets
Rime
also English poetry; French poetry; etc.
also subhead Poetry under various subjects, e.g. Memorial day—Poetry

Appreciation
Helping children enjoy poetry. M. H. Arbuthnot. il Wilson Lib Bul 36:377 Ja '62
What modern writers forget. S. Spender. il Sat R 45:15-17+ Ja 20 '62

Bibliography
All's well in the world of verse. J. Slater. Sat R 44:29-30+ My 6 '61
Books about poetry. R. H. Viguers. Horn Bk 37:141 Ap '61
Clutch of creeds. S. Hazo. Commonweal 75:346-7 D 22 '61
Ear and inner eye of the muse. D. Fitts. il Sat R 45:22-4 Ag 4 '62
From mind to image to meter. J. M. Brinnin. Sat R 44:24-6 N '61
Life guide. Life 52:12 Mr 30 '62
Muse of many voices. R. D. Spector. Sat R 44:15-17+ Jl 22 '61
New books. S. Kunitz. Harper 223:86-91 Ag '61
New poetry. P. Davison. Atlan 210:85-8 N '62
Recent contours of the muse. W. V. O'Connor. Sat R 45:68-71+ Ja 6 '62
Recent poetry. Christian Cent 78:248-9 F 22 '61
Twelve from small presses. X. J. Kennedy. Poetry 99:313-19 F '62
Verse (cont) New Yorker 37:118+ Ja 30; 38:175 Mr 24; 238+ N 17 '62

Collections
See Anthologies

Readers' Guide to Periodical Literature contains, under a variety of subject headings, references to poetry and poets. If the student uses a subject heading not used by the index compilers, he is directed by a cross reference to the subject heading used. Numerous see-also references lead to related material.

Teachers may wish to explain a sample entry:

POETRY

For a wider view of poetry. S. Spender. il Sat R 45:19–21+ My 19 '62

POETRY	Subject heading
For a wider view of poetry	Title of article
S. Spender	Author
il	Illustrated
Sat R	Title of magazine (*Saturday Review*)
45	Volume number
19–21+	Page numbers, continued
My 19 '62	Date (May 19, 1962)

Abbreviations, signs, and symbols are fully explained in the preface. Since the sequence used is standard, students can readily learn to use this well-known index.

Brewtons' *Index to Children's Poetry* and its First and Second Supplements are title, subject, and first-line indexes to poetry in collections for children and young people. The title entry is the main entry and gives the fullest information. All entries are contained in a single alphabetic arrangement. The original index, 1942, indexes about 15,000 poems by more than 2500 authors under more than 1800 subject headings; the first supplement, 1954, indexes additional collections

ANALYSIS OF BOOKS

Nash, Ogden, ed. Moon is shining bright as day; an anthology of good-humored verse; il. by Rose Shirvanian. Lippincott 1953 (1-6)
Contents: 180 poems by 93 authors grouped as follows: Introductory poem, 1 Has anybody seen my mouse? 64; Blum, blum, blum, 40; Over in the meadow, 30; How many miles to Babylon? 9; Four and twenty bowmen, 13; and Yonder see the morning blink, 23. Also Foreword. Indexed by authors, first lines, and titles.

Opie, Iona and Opie, Peter, comps. Oxford nursery rhyme book; with additional illustrations by Joan Hassall. Oxford 1955 (k-3)
Contents: 800 nursery rhymes grouped as follows: Baby games and lullabies, 128; First favourites, 126; Little songs, 93; People, 95; A little learning, 88; Awakening, 76; Wonders, 59; Riddles, tricks, and trippers, 78; and Ballads and songs, 57. Also Preface; Sources of the illustrations. Indexed by first lines, refrains, and familiar titles.

Parker, Elinor, comp. 100 more story poems; il. by Peter Spier. Crowell 1960 (6-12)
Contents: 100 poems by 67 authors grouped as follows: Just for fun, 25; Ballads old and new, 13; Battles long ago, 9; Rogues and heroes, 12; My true love hath my heart, 8; Fantasy and enchantment, 13; Birds and beasts, 11; and Christmastide, 9. Indexed by authors, first lines, and titles.

Parker, Elinor, comp. Singing and the gold; poems translated from world literature; wood engravings by Clare Leighton. Crowell 1962 (7-12)
Contents: 205 poems by 118 authors translated from 34 languages by 107 translators grouped as follows: How sleep the brave, 8; Friendship is a sheltering tree, 9; Arise, my love, my fair one, 56; Sing a song of seasons, 46; Charm me asleep, 32; The bliss of solitude, 35; and All glorious above, 19. Also Foreword. Indexed by authors and sources, first lines, languages, titles, and translators.

Peterson, Isabel J. comp. First book of poetry; il. by Kathleen Elgin. Watts, F. 1954 (k-6)
Contents: 81 poems by 48 authors grouped as follows: A variety of animals, 18; Interesting people, 13; Journeying far and wide, 7; The land of make-believe, 8; The world around us, 15; From season to season, 11; and Just for fun, 9. Also About poetry. Indexed by authors, first lines, and titles.

Plotz, Helen, comp. Imagination's other place; poems of science and mathematics; il. with wood engravings by Clare Leighton. Crowell 1955 (7-12)
Contents: 124 poems by 79 authors grouped as follows: In the beginning, 38; The kingdom of number, 26; Both man and bird and beast, 38; and Watchers of the skies, 22. Also Preface and sectional introductions. Indexed by authors, first lines, and titles.

Plotz, Helen, comp. Untune the sky; poems of music and the dance; il. with wood engravings by Clare Leighton. Crowell 1957 (7-12)
Contents: 134 poems by 105 authors grouped as follows: All instruments, 38; Singing over the earth, 21; One God is God of both, 23; Poet to dancer, 23; and Music shall untune the sky, 29. Also Preface and sectional introductions. Indexed by authors, first lines, and titles.

Read, Herbert, comp. This way, delight; a book of poetry for the young; il. by Juliet Kepes. Pantheon 1956 (5-9)
Contents: 110 poems by 56 authors grouped as follows: Charms, 27; Songs, 43; Enchantments, 23; Escapes, 10; and Stories, 7. Also What is poetry? Indexed by authors and first lines.

Reeves, James. Blackbird in the lilac; verses for children; il. by Edward Ardizzone. Dutton 1959 (1-4)
Contents: 53 poems grouped as follows: The blackbird in the lilac, 1; Dance and rhyme, 12; Hedge and harvest, 10; Elm trees and other people, 11; The street musician, 9; Myths and wonders, 9; and Time to go home, 1.

published between 1938 and 1951; the second supplement, 1965, indexes 85 more collections published between 1949 and 1963. Directions for use, key to abbreviations, and key to symbols for books indexed precede the main index. Also part of the preface is an excellent listing, an analysis of the books indexed; the annotations on the various titles should help the teacher and the student who seek help before purchasing anthologies of poetry.

SECOND SUPPLEMENT   209

Lagerkvist, Pär
"Beauty is most at twilight's close." *PaS*
"A laird, a lord." Mother Goose. *OpO*
The lake isle of Innisfree. William Butler
    Yeats. *FeF—JoAc*
Lakes
    Daddy fell into the pond. A. Noyes. *CoH*
    —FeF
    Down by the pond. A. A. Milne. *MiWc*
    From the mailboat passing by. D. McCord.
    McFf
    The pond. A. von Droste-Hülshoff. *PaS*
    Something better. D. McCord. *McFf*
The **lama.** Ogden Nash. *CoH—FeF—LoL*
    "The one-l lama." *SmLg*
Lamb, Charles
    The old familiar faces. *HaP*
    The snail. *NaM—UnG*
    The triumph of the whale. *PlI* (sel.)
Lamb, Mary
    The child and the snake. *DeT*
    The dessert. *DeT*
The **lamb.** William Blake. *DoP—FeF—*
    JoAc—McW—SmLg—UnG
    Little lamb. *HuSv*
"**Lamb** of God, I look to Thee." See My
    example
Lambdin, Sylvia S.
    January. *HaY*
Lambert, James H., Jr
    The tale of a dog. *CoI*
Lambs. See also Sheep
    The first lamb. E. Farjeon. *FaCb—FaN*
    The lamb. W. Blake. *DoP FeF JoAc*
    McW—SmLg—UnG
    Little lamb. *HuSv*
    Lambs. K. Tynan. *DeT*
    The little young lambs. P. R. Chalmers.
    HuL-2
    "Mary had a little lamb (her father)." Un-
    known. *MoY*
    Mary's lamb. S. J. Hale. *FeF—JoAc—*
    OpO—UnG
    "Mary had a little lamb." *BrL-k—*
    DeMg—LiL
    The pet lamb. W. Wordsworth. *DeT* (sel.)
    Sheep and lambs. K. Tynan. *DoP*
    "Two young lambs." E. Farjeon. *FaCb—*
    FaN
    Woolly lambkins. C. G. Rossetti. *HuSv*
    Young lambs. J. Clare. *UnG*
    "Young lambs to sell. Young lambs to
    sell." Mother Goose. *DeMg*
    The toy lamb seller. *OpO*
Lambs. Katharine Tynan. *DeT*
The **lament** of the white mouse. E. V. Rieu.
    RiF
Laments. See also Death
    Adonais. P. B. Shelley. *HaP* (sel.)
    "Call for the robin-redbreast and the wren."
    From The white devil. J. Webster. *SmLg*
    A dirge. *ReT*
    Coronach. From The lady of the lake. W.
    Scott. *HoW*
    The cowboy's lament. Unknown. *McW—*
    UnMc
    Dirge ("1-2-3 was the number he played
    but today the number came 3-2-1") K.
    Fearing. *HaP*

A dirge ("Rough wind, that moanest loud")
    P. B. Shelley. *HoW*
Dirge ("We do lie beneath the grass")
    T. L. Beddoes. *HoW*
Dirge in woods. G. Meredith. *HoW*
Elegy. C. Tichborne. *HaP*
    The spring is past. *DeT* (sel.)
Elegy for Lucy Lloyd. L. Goch. *PaS*
Elegy on the death of a mad dog. From
    The vicar of Wakefield. O. Goldsmith.
    HaP—McW—SmLg—UnMc
Elegy written in a country churchyard. T.
    Gray. *DeT—HaP*
"Full fathom five thy father lies." From
    The tempest. W. Shakespeare. *SmLg*
    Ariel's dirge. *NaE—ReT*
The ghost's lament. Unknown. *MaB*
    The ghost's song. *SmLg*
The lament of the white mouse. E. V. Rieu.
    RiF
A lyke-wake dirge. Unknown. *MaB—NaE*
Requiem. R. L. Stevenson. *HaP—McW—*
    ThP—UnG
The sea-ritual. G. Darley. *HoW*
Song on the water. T. L. Beddoes. *SmLg*
The sparrow's dirge. J. Skelton. *SmLg*
"Wake all the dead, what ho, what ho."
    W. Davenant. *SmLg*
Lamplighter barn. Myra Cohn Livingston.
    LiWa
Lamplighters
    "Light the lamps up, lamplighter." E.
    Farjeon. *BrS—HuL-2*
Lampson, Frederick Locker. See Locker-
    Lampson, Frederick
"Lancaster bore him such a little town."
    See A hundred collars
Lancelot, Sir (Lancelot du Lac) (about)
    The lady of Shalott. A. Tennyson. *HoW—*
    UnMg
"**Land** lies in water, it is shadowed green."
    See The map
The **land** of counterpane. Robert Louis
    Stevenson. *FeF—HuSv—JoAc—NaE*
The **land** of Ho-Ho-Hum. William Jay
    Smith. *SmL*
The **land** of Nod. Robert Louis Stevenson.
    UnG
"**Land** of our birth, we pledge to thee." See
    The children's song
The **land** of story-books. Robert Louis
    Stevenson. *ArTp—FeF—UnG*
"The **land** was ours before we were the
    land's." See The gift outright
"The **land** was white." Mother Goose. *OpO*
The **land** where hate should die. Denis A.
    McCarthy. *BrL-8*
The **landing** of the Pilgrim Fathers. Felicia
    Dorothea Hemans. *ArTp—BrR-5—FeF*
    —UnG
Landor, Walter Savage
    I strove with none. *HaP*
    Leofric and Godiva. *GrCc*
    On music. *GrCc*
    On the death of Ianthe. *GrCc*
    Past ruined Ilion. *HaP*
Landscape ("I want to write a book of
    chaste and simple verse") Charles
    Baudelaire, tr. fr. the French by George
    Dillon. *PaS*

Teaching Literature to Adolescents

Since its initial publication in 1948, Benét's *Reader's Encyclopedia* has been one of the most popular and useful reference books in the field of literature. Allusions and references in writings from ancient times to the present are explained. In a single alphabet, the book identifies authors, titles of literary works, literary characters, literary movements; terms used in science, philosophy, music, art; highlights of history, mythology. In short, most subjects important to readers of books are touched upon. For the new edition, all old entries were re-evaluated; many, especially those covering world literature, were expanded.

Title page of Thomas Niccol's translation of Thucydides' *History of the Peloponnesian Wars* (1550).

Hence, the thugs became a professional fraternity of stranglers who supported themselves by the plunder obtained from those they strangled. Their native name is *p'hansigars* ("stranglers"); that of *thug* ("cheat") was given them in 1810. Their methods were rigorously suppressed under British rule, and they were practically extinct by 1840. The word is now used in English for any ruffian.

Thule. The ancient name of an island or point of land 6 days' sail north of Britain. It was considered to be the extreme northern limit of the world. The name is first found in the account by Polybius (c. 150 B.C.) of the voyage made by Pytheas in the late fourth century B.C. Pliny says, "It is an island in the Northern Ocean discovered by Pytheas, after sailing six days from the Orcades." Others consider it to be Shetland, in which opinion they agree with the descriptions of Ptolemy and Tacitus. Still others assert that it was some part of the coast of Norway. The etymology of the name is unknown. Ultima Thule means the end of the world, the last extremity.

Tibi serviat Ultima Thule.
Vergil, *Georgics*, i, 30

thumbs down (Lat., *pollice verso*). A sign ordering death for a fallen gladiator. At the gladiatorial contests in ancient Rome, the winning gladiator turned to the spectators to ask whether he should kill his fallen enemy. If the spectators held out their arms with thumbs down, the victim must die; thumbs up meant that he was to be spared.

Thundertentronckh, Arminius von. A pseudonym under which Matthew ARNOLD wrote a number of satiric essays, chiefly for *The Pall Mall Gazette*. They were brought together in book form under the title *Friendship's Garland* (1871).

Thurber, James [Grover] (1894-1961). American essayist, short-story writer, and humorist. Thurber began his career as a journalist; in 1927, he met E. B. White, who introduced him to Harold Ross, the editor of a newly founded magazine, *The New Yorker*. During Thurber's years as a staff member he did much to establish the tone, style, and popularity of the magazine. Thurber turned his humor, his satire, and his irony on the follies of men and women, which he revealed in his lucid prose and inimitable drawings; nevertheless, he affirmed the power of love in a fantastic, often nightmarish world. His story *The Secret Life of Walter Mitty*, later made into a movie, describes the fantasies of a Caspar Milquetoast who imagines himself a hero. Among Thurber's other works are *Is Sex Necessary?* (1929), with E. B. White; *The Seal in the Bedroom and Other Predicaments* (1932); *The Middle-Aged Man on the Flying Trapeze* (1935); *Let Your Mind Alone* (1937); *The Male Animal* (1940), a play with Elliot Nugent; *Fables for Our Times* (1940); *The Thurber Carnival* (1945); *Alarms and Diversions* (1957); and *The Years with Ross* (1959), a memoir of Ross. *Lanterns and Lances* (1961) is a book of essays; *Credos and Curios* (1962) was published posthumously.

Thurio. In Shakespeare's TWO GENTLEMEN OF VERONA, Valentine's foolish, homely rival for the hand of Silvia. When the cowardly Thurio disavows his love for her in the face of danger, the duke of Milan, Silvia's father, consents to her marrying Valentine.

Thurso's Landing (1932). A narrative poem by Robinson JEFFERS. The poem deals with Helen Thurso's ambivalent attitudes toward her husband, whom she alternately loves and hates; toward her crippled brother-in-law, who loves her; and toward death itself, which simultaneously fascinates and repels her.

Thurston, E[rnest] Temple (1879-1933). English novelist and playwright. Among his sentimental novels are *The City of Beautiful Nonsense* (1909) and *Richard Furlong* (1913); among his plays, *The Wandering Jew* (1920) and *Charmeuse* (1930). He was at one time married to the novelist Katherine Cecil THURSTON.

Thurston, Katherine Cecil (1875-1911). English novelist. She was at one time the wife of E. Temple THURSTON. Her book *John Chilcote, M. P.* (1904; U.S. title, *The Masquerader*) was a best seller.

Thus Spake Zarathustra (Also sprach Zarathustra; 1883-1892). A philosophical narrative by Friedrich NIETZSCHE in which the ancient Persian philosopher Zarathustra (see ZOROASTER) is used as a mouthpiece for the author's views. In it, Nietzsche develops his doctrine of the ÜBERMENSCH, and the

238   CHARACTER   CHARACTER

1
Zealous, yet modest; innocent, though free;
Patient of toil; serene amidst alarms;
Inflexible in faith; invincible in arms.
  JAMES BEATTIE, *The Minstrel*. Bk. i, st. 11.

2
With more capacity for love than earth
Bestows on most of mortal mould and birth,
His early dreams of good out-stripp'd the
    truth,
And troubled manhood follow'd baffled youth.
  BYRON, *Lara*. Canto i, st. 18.

3
The ideal of courtesy, wit, grace, and charm.
(Specimen fuisse humanitatis, salis, suavita-
tis, leporis.)
  CICERO, *Tusculanarum Disputationum*. Bk. v,
    ch. 19, sec. 55

4
A man of letters, manners, morals, parts.
  COWPER, *Tirocinium*, l. 673

5
Even children follow'd with endearing wile,
And pluck'd his gown, to share the good
    man's smile.
  GOLDSMITH, *The Deserted Village*, l. 183.

6
A nice unparticular man.

13
Free from self-seeking, envy, low design,
I have not found a whiter soul than thine.
  CHARLES LAMB, *To Martin Charles Burney*.

14
Other hope had she none, nor wish in life,
    but to follow
Meekly, with reverent steps, the sacred feet
    of her Saviour.
  LONGFELLOW, *Evangeline*. Pt. ii, sec. 5, l. 35.

15
His magic was not far to seek,—
He was so human! Whether strong or weak,
Far from his kind he neither sank nor soared,
But sate an equal guest at every board:
No beggar ever felt him condescend,
No prince presume; for still himself he bare
At manhood's simple level, and where'er
He met a stranger, there he left a friend.
  J. R. LOWELL, *Agassiz*. Pt. ii, sec. 2.

16
The wisest man could ask no more of Fate
Than to be simple, modest, manly, true,
Safe from the Many, honored by the Few;
To count as naught in World, or Church, or
    State,
But inwardly in secret to be great.

Stevenson's *Home Book of Quotations* contains more than 50,000 quotations by nearly 5000 authors. The book is arranged alphabetically by subject with subarrangement by smaller topics. Students searching for a topic not found in alphabetical sequence in the body of the work should use the index, which leads either to the synonymous term used or to the larger topic under which the subject can be found. Most often the index uses nouns as its key words from quotations; sometimes, however, adjectives and adverbs are used. This is a comprehensive, well-chosen collection, especially useful in identifying fragments of quotations.

2444   BEGGAR   BELL

Beggar, *continued*
  better to die a b. than live
    a b. 145: 1
  drunk as a b. 501:13
  how a b. should be an-
    swer'd 146: 3
  in the midst of plenty ..1571:18
  in the midst of wealth 1333:15
  jealous of b. 1536:18
  king a b. now play done 1038:21
  long-remembered b. 145: 3
  no b. ever felt him con-
    descend 238:15
  on horseback 145:21
  one b. bideth woe 145: 5
  pleases me 145:16
  prepares to plunge 15:10
  scratch b. before you die 1770:10
  shameless b., short denial ..144:16
  squealin' for quarter 332: 2
  stiff-necked, Glasgow b. ..238:12
  sue a b., get a louse 145: 2
  taxed for corner 1695: 2
  that I am, poor in thanks 824:20
  that is dumb, you know 1209:14
  through the world am I ..145:11
  void of care b. trips 1568: 6
  whiles I am a b. I will rail 146: 2
  young courtier, old b. 327: 5
Beggar's book outworths no-
    ble's blood 146: 1
  scrip never filled 146: 5
Beggared all description ..140:10
Beggars: all b. at His gate 145: 4
  and thieves get much 1718:15

Beginnings be but poor and
    low 1244: 8
  from small b. grow 104:13
  of all things small 146: 9
  of evil small 146:15
  resist b. 146:15
Begins: whatever b. also ends 147:17
Beglückte: Das Glück erhebe
    billig der B. 711:17
Begot: when they b. me 646: 1
Begs: never b. seldom eats 1064: 4
  the simplest questions 100: 5
  to be desir'd to give 777:14
Beguile: fashioned to b. ..2201: 3
  many 421: 7
  the thing I am 1078: 6
Begun: things bad b. 147: 4
  well b., half done 146: 7
Behave yoursel' before folk 150: 4
Behaved ourselves well 149: 5
Behaves: he doesn't act; he b. 9: 1
Behavior 148
  as the occasion, so the b. ..148: 8
  during good b. 149: 7
  fair b. in thee 149: 4
  finest of the fine arts 148:11
  garment of the mind 148: 5
  her evil b. 1829:11
  is a mirror 148:13
  is to retain dignity 148: 4
  laws of b. yield to energy ..148:11
  learn b. one of another ..148: 6
  loose b. I throw off 1686: 6
  loved so well high b. 149:10
  men's b. like apparel ...148: 5

Beliefs: bears b. as tree
    bears apples 151: 7
  depend on where we are
    born 1428:22
  determined by character ..1380:14
  lifeless old b. 69: 9
  not b'lieve 'em tu hard ..1919:12
  strong b. win strong men 151: 1
Believable because unbe-
    lievable 152:14
Believe all I can under-
    stand 1691:15
  always ready to b. 334:11
  and ye shall receive 1583:4a
  because it is impossible ..152:14
  do not b. hastily 152: 3
  easier to b. than doubt ..152: 1
  everything one hears 1408:13
  first you don't b. 151: 2
  have to b. in happiness ..857: 8
  her though I know she lies 1205: 3
  I b. in God 795:11
  in equality of man 801:17
  in order to reason 1678:10
  learn nothing but to b. ..2068:15
  Lord, I b. 151:17
  most potently b. 35:16
  no force compel to b. 151: 4
  one who knows 1389: 5
  only b. what I understand 151: 6
  powerfully and potently b. ..35:16
  those whom we do not
    know 2046:1-1
  to b. better than to compre-
    hend 797: 9